D0830730

GOVERNMENT RULES INDUSTRY

A STUDY OF THE NRA

GOVERNMENT RULES INDUSTRY

A STUDY OF THE NRA

BY
MICHAEL F. GALLAGHER
LECTURER AT JOHN MARSHALL LAW SCHOOL OF CHICAGO

Every generation needs to be addressed in its own language. —BOSANQUET.

NEW YORK
OXFORD UNIVERSITY PRESS
1934

FIRST EDITION

PRINTED IN THE UNITED STATES OF AMERICA

To

E. G.

FOREWORD

THIS volume is the sequel to a course of lectures given in April, 1934, to a group of advanced law students and lawyers. The original material was received with such generous interest that I have been led, with a temerity which I shall probably repent, to revise and expand the text to the dimensions of a book for general readers. If the result has any wide appeal it will be due, I need hardly say, to the timeliness and critical importance of the subject rather than to any originality in thought or merit in composition. More than 15,000,000 workers now have their daily occupations governed by Codes of Fair Competition.

One peril of publication is that many of the paragraphs may become obsolete before they leave the press. The background of conditions and events is changing with startling rapidity. The NRA is actively and energetically functioning, doing daily an astounding amount of work. New executive and administrative orders, new legislation or judicial decisions, might any day require a change of the text. The book deals with a phase of a dynamic movement, marked by vast and wholly unprecedented government action. New laws creating new powers, new boards, commissions and agencies, new executive and administrative decrees, new methods and experiments, sudden decisions and reversals of decisions, are every day transpiring, a swiftly moving sweep of events and, under the surface, there are deeper currents of social and economic change which may be moulding a new civilization.

"Great economic and social forces," said Viscount Morley, writing during another era of convulsive industrial changes, "flow with tidal sweep over communities only half conscious of that which is befalling them. Wise statesmen are those who foresee what time is thus bringing, and try to shape institutions and to mould men's thoughts and purpose in accordance with the change that is silently surrounding them."[1]

It is not using a mere rhetorical phrase to say that the Constitution is on trial. Its restraints and limitations on legislative and executive action are under strain and test from which they will emerge either inert and innocuous or with renewed vitality and vigor.

Will the Federal Government remain in truth one of special and enumerated powers?

Will it be content to function within its granted powers?

Will constitutional restraints and limitations remain basic elements of law with dynamic force actually governing society or mere formal declarations?

Can constitutional restraints and limitations be so construed and applied as not to be a barrier to welfare and justice and progress?

These questions will be answered by the decisions of the Supreme Court of the United States in dealing with the multiform legislation embraced within the New Deal. The most significant of these decisions will be those that deal with the basic constitutional validity of the provisions of the National Industrial Recovery Act.

Basic law is in the throes of a social conflict. This conflict is not new but recently in the maze of new social and economic legislation it has assumed in the judicial forum an acute intensity. Issues are clearly defined and fateful decisions cannot be avoided. In the common law of England, as in its life and literature, there is a strain of virile individualism. Many of the great constitutional

[1] *Life of Cobden,* by Viscount Morley, page 472. Macmillan.

principles of that country were evolved in protest against undue interferences and exactions of government. Transplanted to the free soil of America the ideas of the rightful independence of the individual lived and grew in even greater vigor. Sacredness of private ownership of property, sanctity of obligations under contracts, liberty of action in making contracts and in business enterprises, freedom of speech and of the press, are affirmations enshrined in our law. Hitherto the vindication of these principles has been the chief function of the judicial power. Now in sharp conflict with this individualism is the legal theory based on the paramount test of social justice and social desirability. It conceives government as having something akin to supreme unlimited power to legislate for human welfare. Its thesis is that individual liberty, private property rights, and freedom of action in business enterprise, must yield to legislation designed for general welfare and social justice. To this school the Bill of Rights is a myth and the Magna Charta a legend. Under its influence forensic argument has ceased to be a mere battery of legal analogies and now is often a searching and profound study of the social and economic conditions under and by reason of which the power of government has been exerted. "It is possible," again to quote Morley, "to be an economist without being a statesman, but you cannot be a statesman without being an economist."[2] Great jurists today must be sociologists and economists.

Indestructible rights and liberty of the individual versus imperative social and economic justice and necessity — this is the conflict on which battles are being fought involving grave issues. Hardly a week passes that this fundamental conflict is not in argument at the bar of

[2] *Recollections,* by Viscount Morley, Vol. 1, p. 138. Macmillan.

the Supreme Court, now profoundly aware, to quote Mr. Chief Justice Hughes, "of the necessity of finding ground for a rational compromise between individual rights and public welfare."[3] A perfect compromise will remain an unattainable ideal, but in the efforts gradually to achieve a working compromise between the rights and liberty of the citizen, on the one hand, and legislative and executive action and control, on the other, judicial decisions with respect to the NIRA will be of creative importance. They will announce the doctrines by which our future social and economic life will be governed.

The NRA is the most colossal creation of the New Deal. Its place in the recovery program of the government is preëminent. National in scope, embracing all trade and industry, it asserts a detailed regulative control over economic life never before attempted by a government organized upon a democratic basis. In its councils social forces are battling for domination. The NRA is the arbiter of the destiny of capital and labor. Yet the Supreme Court by one blow may strike it down. At no juncture in our history has the application of the Constitution by the Supreme Court been of more profound and dramatic interest.

The purpose of this book is to describe the NRA in structure and in action and to apply to it the principles of the Federal Constitution. This will require an analysis and interpretation of the objectives and provisions of the Recovery Act, and a survey of the administrative organization and procedure of the NRA, the process of code-making, and the validity of codes. Title II of the NIRA will be considered in an analysis of the taxing and spending power of Congress. The basic legal

[3] *Home Building & Loan Assn.* v. *Blaisdell* (Minnesota Mortgage Moratorium case), 290 U. S. 398, at 442 (1933).

and constitutional questions will be developed. While these discussions will deal with law and its administration, it will be perfectly apparent that this is in no sense a legal treatise or text-book. Technical niceties in legal distinctions are purposely avoided. The constitutional problems are perforce revealed in broad outline and by large and bold strokes. If these chapters illumine the way to a clearer view of the NRA in its relation to law and the Constitution, their purpose will be fulfilled.

I acknowledge my deep indebtedness to Mr. Samuel W. Witwer and Mr. Ralph E. Webb, two young Chicago lawyers, for their invaluable aid in required investigations and in the correction of the manuscript and proofs. A large portion of the labor in preparing the index has been done by my daughter, Mrs. Charles A. Butland, and my son, David, and I wish here to record my appreciation of their work. Mr. Earl B. Wilkinson and Mr. Samuel M. Rinaker, of the Chicago Bar, have read all of the material and have made suggestions of which I have availed myself and this assistance I gratefully acknowledge. For the comment and opinions expressed in the book I assume sole responsibility.

M. F. G.

CONTENTS

CHAPTER I

NATIONAL INDUSTRIAL RECOVERY ACT—ITS OBJECTIVES AND PROVISIONS

ECONOMIC and financial conditions in the Spring of 1933 entirely justified emergency action by the Government. The banking crisis had come and gone leaving in its wake a confused and anxious nation. Normal commercial intercourse was almost suspended. The economic structure had been wrenched and shaken. The idleness of 12,000,000 workers had spread through the country dire want and unrest. Vague fears were in the air of further unknown disasters, if not of a complete collapse. One hope and faith survived and that was in the magic power of legislation. The exertion in fullest measure of the remedial powers of legislation was without question the desire and expectation of the people. It was no time to philosophize as to the just and proper sphere of constituted authority, to measure closely granted powers, to ponder on constitutional principles and limitations. Such reflections and deliberations were indeed appropriate but they were not of the temper of the times. The hour had struck for action, for the most effective, comprehensive and vigorous legislative and executive action that could be devised. The people had heard the promise of the New Deal and they wanted it fulfilled.

The Seventy-Third Congress, assembled in special session, answering the successive appeals of a President who voiced the preponderant thought and feeling of the country, promptly enacted into law an array of measures unparalleled for originality and boldness. This legislative program embraced enactments designed to meet various phases of the crisis and to promote economic recovery by achieving sundry definite ends. Of these statutes two were of overshadowing importance, the Agricultural Adjustment Act (basis of AAA) and the National Industrial Recovery Act (basis of NRA). Farm legislation was generally regarded as designed to aid a class, having as its cardinal purpose the achievement of a parity in prices between farm products and other commodities. The National Industrial Recovery Act, as its title implied, was addressed to the whole economic and commercial system. It was the supreme legislative effort for rehabilitation of trade and industry. Of this statute the President, in affixing his signature on June 16, 1933, declared:

> "History probably will regard the National Industrial Recovery Act as the most important and far reaching legislation ever enacted by the American Congress."

Subsequent events in the application of the law have demonstrated that this statement of the President was sober truth and not made under emotional stress of the economic crisis. Measured by its effect on the lives, occupations and fortunes of the people, this statute is supreme in our legal and economic history. Hitherto the government had intervened in business in a piecemeal and isolated fashion. By this statute it embraces within its collective control all trade and industry. In the scope and measure and detail of its regulation the statute is novel and drastic. The legal concept of a "business affected with a public interest" has been expanded to include every trade and business. It not only permits but requires coöperation by industrial and trade groups to an extent which theretofore had been regarded as criminal under the anti-trust laws and as illegal under the historic doctrines of the common law applying to monopolies and restraints of trade. It has been hailed as a Magna Charta of business coöperation, yet at the same time it gives the President a degree of power over business unparalleled in previous peace-time history of the country or even during war. It sanctions, encourages and promotes trade unionism and collective bargaining and at the same time gives ultimate authority over wages and hours to the President. It is by far the most important enactment in the history of American labor legislation, but at the same time its provisions which liberate industry from the restraints of the anti-trust laws will be found equally significant and important. It lodges in a department of the government the vast and intricate job of regulating all of the trade and industry in the country. This is a task so colossal and of such infinite detail as to stagger the imagination and inevitably to suggest to thoughtful minds the inquiry: Is it humanly possible?

It will be necessary to review in rather tedious detail the provisions of this extraordinary statute as a basis of later discussion. In doing so we must have in mind that it is emergency legislation. Only in the impelling stress of a grave economic emergency could the successive sections of this measure be deemed necessary. The emergency character of the legislation is fixed by the law itself. All agencies established under the Act cease to exist at the expiration of two years from the date of its enactment, that is, June 16, 1935, or sooner if the President shall by proclamation, or Congress by joint resolution, declare that the emergency has ended.

The title of the Act is very broad. It is entitled: AN ACT TO ENCOURAGE NATIONAL INDUSTRIAL RECOVERY, TO FOSTER FAIR COMPETITION AND TO PROVIDE FOR THE

CONSTRUCTION OF CERTAIN USEFUL PUBLIC WORKS, AND FOR OTHER PURPOSES.

The statute is made up of three Titles:

Title I embraces the provisions dealing with Industrial Recovery;
Title II deals with Public Works and Construction Projects; and
Title III with Amendments to Emergency Relief and Construction Act, and Miscellaneous Provisions.

Title III is not germane to the purpose of this book. Title II, authorizing an appropriation of 3 and 3/10 billion dollars for the financing of public works, is a separate piece of legislation, which will later be considered.

Title I, which refers to industrial recovery, is the portion of the statute which now engages our attention.

Section 1 of Title I is a declaration of policy. Such a declaration of policy in any statute is unusual. Its expressed purpose was to furnish to the courts the basis and reasons for the Act. It declares the intentions of Congress rather than to leave to the judicial department the exploration of such intentions.

The first sentence of Section 1 of Title I is a legislative declaration of the existence of the emergency. It reads:

"A national emergency productive of widespread unemployment and disorganization of industry, which burdens interstate and foreign commerce, affects the public welfare, and undermines the standards of living of the American people, is hereby declared to exist."

The existence and gravity of the emergency which led to the passage of the Act is no longer open to question. Its existence has been declared and its character defined by legislative enactment. It involved widespread unemployment and disorganization of industry; it burdened interstate and foreign commerce; it affected the public welfare; it undermined the standards of living of the American people.

To meet this emergency Congress enacted the law. Section 1 lays down its objectives. This is a broad recital of the great and ambitious purposes which Congress was seeking to achieve. As enumerated in the law they are:

To remove obstructions to the free flow of interstate and foreign commerce which tend to diminish the amount thereof;
To provide for the general welfare by promoting the organization of industry for the purpose of coöperative action among trade groups;
To induce and maintain united action of labor and management under adequate governmental sanctions and supervision;
To eliminate unfair competitive practices;
To promote the fullest possible utilization of the present productive capacity of industries;
To avoid undue restriction of production (except as may be temporarily required);
To increase the consumption of industrial and agricultural products by increasing purchasing power;
To reduce and relieve unemployment;
To improve standards of labor; and otherwise to rehabilitate industry and to conserve natural resources.

These are the purposes of the law and the succeeding provisions deal with the machinery for their accomplishment.

Section 2 deals with administration. Plenary power in the creation and utilization of necessary agencies is vested in the President. He is authorized to establish such agencies, to accept and utilize voluntary and uncompensated services, to appoint, without regard to the provisions of the civil service laws, officers and employees, and to utilize such federal officers and employees, and, with the consent of the State, such state and local officers and employees, as he may find necessary, and to prescribe their duties.

Delegation of all the functions and powers of the President is authorized without restriction. By the language of the Act the President may delegate any of his functions and powers to such officers, agents and employees as he may designate or appoint, and he may establish an industrial planning and research agency to aid in carrying out his functions. The importance of this provision granting an unrestricted power to the President to delegate his functions and powers will be apparent as we discuss the succeeding provisions of the law. Under this authority the President established the National Recovery Administration — the NRA. From the same legal source is drawn the position and vast authority which has been exercised by the Administrator, General Hugh S. Johnson.

Beginning with Section 3, the statute provides the five great methods for its application and enforcement. Briefly, they are:

Voluntary trade and industry codes.
Voluntary agreements within an industry.
Limited codes, — that is, codes limited to the subjects of hours of labor, wages and working conditions.
Compulsory codes imposed by the President.
A system of licensing to be used in extreme cases where evils are shown to exist.

Voluntary trade and industry codes are the central idea of the whole legislative scheme. Section 3 deals with the procedure for the formation of these codes. The initiative is taken by trade and industrial associations or groups. These groups frame and submit to the NRA a tentative code for the trade or industry. These codes cover a wide range of industrial and trade activities. If approved by the NRA, and then by the President, they become codes of fair competition for the trades or industries, represented by the applicant or applicants. The President is authorized to approve such codes if he finds: (1) that the applicants for a code impose no inequitable restrictions to membership; (2) that the applicants are truly representative of the trade or industries for which they speak; (3) that such proposed codes are not designed to promote monopolies or to eliminate or oppress small enterprises, and will not operate to discriminate against the latter; (4) that the proposed codes will, in his judgment, tend to effectuate the policy of the law.

All persons affected by a code are entitled to a hearing before its approval by the President. The President may impose as a condition of his approval such requirements as to the making of reports and the keeping of accounts as he believes necessary for the protection of consumers, competitors, employees, and others, and may make such exceptions to and exemptions from the provisions of a code as he deems necessary to effectuate the policy declared in the statute.

By Section 3 it is provided that after the President has approved any code its provisions shall be the standards of fair competition for the particular trade or industry or subdivision thereof, and that any violation of such standards in or affecting interstate or foreign commerce shall be deemed an unfair method of competition in commerce under the terms of the Federal Trade Commission Act.

The law specifically invests the District Courts of the

United States with jurisdiction to prevent and restrain violations of the codes and also makes any violation of code provisions a misdemeanor punishable by a fine of not more than $500 for each offense. Each day the violation continues is deemed a separate offense.

A voluntary code of fair competition for any trade or industry has two aspects. It is a contract between those who accept and assent to the code, on the one hand, and the government of the United States, on the other. It also has the force of law and is in fact a criminal statute.

While a code is a contract between the assenting members of the trade or industry and the government, it is plainly more than that, because, when approved by the President and promulgated, it is binding upon the whole trade or industry even though certain units of that industry were not represented in the formation of the code. The law is clear that after the President shall have approved any such code its provisions shall be the standards of fair competition for the whole trade or industry, and in dealing with the operation and binding effect of the code the statute makes no distinction between intrastate and interstate trade and commerce.

The application for the code may be made in the language of the law by "one or more trade or industrial associations or groups." The decision as to whether or not an association or group making application for a code is truly representative of the trade or industry rests with the President. When the President makes that decision by the acceptance and approval of a code it operates with respect to all and is binding on every dealer or manufacturer, large and small, in every part of the country. It should be noted, however, that where a code affects the service and welfare of persons engaged in other steps of the economic process, such persons have the right to be heard prior to the approval by the President of the code.

In a proceeding for the violation of a code it is no defense that the person charged with such violation did not have notice of the hearing for the formation of the code. In a word, an approved code is binding upon all embraced within the definition of the trade or industry contained in the code, even though a minority of those members fail to agree to the terms of the code.

The codes considered in the preceding paragraphs are voluntary codes. They are the codes drafted by organized industry and submitted to the NRA, finally formed by negotiation and agreement, accepted by the representative organization of the trade or industry, and approved by the President. Other types of codes are, however, provided by the statute and these are of a far more drastic nature. They are involuntary or compulsory codes.

The President is invested with the power upon his own motion, or upon complaint that abuses inimical to the public interest and contrary to the policy declared in the statute are prevalent in any trade or industry not having a code, to prescribe and approve a code of fair competition for such trade or industry. Before the President can promulgate such a code and impose it upon a trade or industry there must be a hearing after notice. Such a code promulgated by the President upon his own motion, or after complaint, shall have the same effect as a Code of Fair Competition initiated and proposed by the trade or industry and approved by the President.

This power of the President to impose upon an industry a code having the force of law is without doubt one of the gravest and most extraordinary powers ever conferred upon an official of government by a free people. All the working conditions in the industry, all of its productive and distributing operations, may in detail be regulated and controlled under such a set of rules, having the force of law, as the President in his sole discretion may prescribe. This is potential dictatorship by statute. Here is the power to dictate the economic life of the whole nation. I am here discussing the *power* vested in the President by the Act. At the time of the writing of these pages this extraordinary power has not been exercised. But while no involuntary code has been imposed, the provisions for codes by compulsion are having a definite influence on the framing of all codes. To many they counsel compromise and concession and submission. They are a Sword of Damocles suspended over the neck of industry.

The indirect effective operation of these compulsory provisions will be clearer from a reading of the first bulletin issued by the NRA under date of June 19, 1933, addressed to all trade associations and industrial and labor groups. It contained this significant paragraph:

"It is the purpose of the Act to encourage a voluntary submission of codes of fair competition and the procedure offered by these provisions for basic codes is intended to simplify and expedite this process. But in the event that codes of fair competition are not voluntarily submitted, attention is invited to other pertinent provisions of the Act. It is provided in section 3 (d) of the Act that the President upon his own motion or if complaint is made, may after public notice and hearing prescribe a code of fair competition for a trade or industry or subdivision thereof."

The power to impose an involuntary or compulsory code upon all trade and industry, when the industry cannot or will not agree upon a voluntary code, and other powers of the President created by the Recovery Act, which I am about to consider, are more vast than were those conferred upon President Wilson for the prosecution of the war.[1] All these powers may without restriction be transferred to other officials of the government. "During these emergency days," Senator Wagner told the House Committee on Ways and Means, "we have got to be generous in our delegation of power, and also trust the individual in the administration."[2]

Another vitally important provision gives the President regulatory powers over imports when, on the basis of an investigation by the Tariff Commission, he believes such regulation necessary to render effective the purposes of codes and agreements made under the Act. He is empowered to lay down conditions upon which goods may be imported, and to limit the quantity of imports if he finds such action necessary to prevent any code or agreement from being rendered ineffective. Importers may be forbidden to import without first obtaining a federal license.

The President may, under such circumstances as he deems sufficient to justify his action, change or cancel customs duties, or limit or forbid imports. His action is final, for the statute reads:

"The decision of the President as to the facts shall be conclusive."

The evident purpose of that section is to protect trade and industry operating under a code from the foreign competition that would make impossible compliance with the provisions of the code as to wages, hours of labor, and other basic working conditions.

[1] Read *Crisis Government,* by Lindsay Rogers, p. 118, *et seq.*
[2] Hearings before Senate Finance Committee, May 22 to June 1, 1933.

Section 4 deals with agreements and licenses by the President. This section authorizes the President to make agreements with and approve voluntary agreements among persons engaged in a trade or industry, labor organizations, and trade and industrial groups, if in his judgment such agreements will aid in accomplishing the purposes of the law. This section originally was of great significance in the grant of power which it gave the President. Under it the President issued his nation-wide invitation to employers to agree with him as to certain working conditions, particularly regarding wages and employment. This was the President's Reëmployment Agreement, popularly called the "Blanket Code," issued July 27, 1933. It had as its legal basis Section 4 (a).

The basic points in the agreement were:

The elimination of child labor;

The limitation of weekly hours of labor under varying circumstances to from 35 to 40 hours;

The fixing of minimum wages, under varying circumstances, at from $12 to $15 by the week, and 30 cents to 40 cents by the hour;

An equitable adjustment upward of wages higher than the minimum;

The limitation of price increases to the amount of increased costs;

The support of enterprises which were parties to the agreement.

The distinction between agreements and codes under the Act should be clearly grasped. Agreements deal almost exclusively with hours of work and rates of pay, while codes cover the entire range of industrial and trade activities.

Section 4 (a) is extremely broad. Almost any type of

agreement between employers and employees, between members of trade groups, between one labor union and another, between one trade group and another, which promotes the policy of the law, to which the President wishes to give the sanction of his approval, may be comprehended within its terms. Its purpose appears to be to facilitate any sort of agreement which may be deemed a desirable supplement to the provisions of codes.

Section 4 (b) is an exceedingly drastic provision. Whenever the President shall find that activities which he believes contrary to the purpose of the law, are being practiced in any trade or industry, the provision confers upon him the power to license business enterprises and to make such license a condition precedent to the carrying on of business. Such action can be taken only after public notice and hearing specified by the President. The statute does not define the activities contrary to its policy. It refers to destructive wage-cutting or price-cutting or other activities. Under this section the President has power to decide what is destructive price-cutting or wage-cutting. He can make his own decision as to what other activities are contrary to the policy of the statute. He can then find that the offenses as defined by him have been committed and upon that finding he can exclude citizens from interstate commerce on such conditions as he in his discretion may determine. The powers vested in the President by this section are an unusual compound of legislative, judicial and executive functions.

Under the licensing power no person shall, after a date fixed in an announcement that a license is required, engage in any business specified in such announcement unless he shall first have obtained a license pursuant to the regulations prescribed. Such a license may be suspended or revoked by the President after hearings if violation of its terms is shown. Any order of the President suspending or revoking any such license shall be final if in accordance with the law. Any person who without a license, or in violation of any of its conditions, carries on any such business for which a license is required, shall, upon conviction, be fined not more than $500 or be imprisoned not more than six months, or both. Each day the violation continues is deemed a separate offense.

By express provision the licensing power of the President expires one year after the date of the enactment of the law. It will, therefore, expire on June 16, 1934, unless extended by act of Congress. Its expiration, however, at that time is somewhat less important in view of the power vested in the President to impose involuntary codes, which continues for the life of the Recovery Act. The licensing power was the ultimate weapon of enforcement granted to the President. It was obviously a power of life or death over business. It was bitterly attacked in Congress and because of such attacks it was limited to a one-year duration.

The licensing power is one more of the great prerogatives of the President created by the Recovery Act which has not at this time been exercised.

The statute then proceeds to deal with the perplexing subject of the anti-trust laws. While Title I of the Act is in effect, and for 60 days thereafter, any code, agreement or license approved, prescribed or issued, and in effect, and any action complying with the provisions thereof taken during such period (that is, during the duration of the code and for 60 days thereafter) is declared exempt from the provisions of the anti-trust laws. These include the Sherman Act of 1890, the Clayton Act and the Federal Trade Commission Act of 1914.

The intention of Congress was to make lawful by codes many agreements which would formerly have been condemned under the anti-trust laws. Code provisions containing in effect covenants to fix prices, limit production, or apportion the market, would under the anti-trust laws be illegal, but, under the new form of coöperation through codes, are, it would appear, safe from legal attack. With respect to all organized effort and coöperation included within or expressly or impliedly authorized by codes, the Sherman law is by Section 5 of the statute suspended in midair. The importance of this phase of the Recovery Act cannot be overstated.

In connection with the provision suspending the anti-trust laws we must again consider that portion of the law before discussed, which provides that codes shall not be approved that are designed to promote monopolies or to eliminate or oppress small enterprises, or discriminate against them, and the express declaration in Section 3 (b) of the Act that "nothing in this title shall be construed to impair the powers of the Federal Trade Commission under such Act, as amended." This refers to a separate statute. The precise significance of these declarations and their consistency is not clear, but in any event they are of influence with the NRA in framing the provisions of codes. The whole subject of the anti-trust laws and the NRA will be treated later in this volume.

Section 6 is of minor importance. It requires that no trade or industrial association or group shall be eligible to receive the benefit of the provisions of the Act until it files with the President a statement containing such information relative to the activities of the association or group as the President shall by regulation prescribe. The President is authorized to prescribe regulations designed to insure that any organization availing itself of the benefits of this title shall be truly representative of the trade or industry represented by such organization. Any organization violating such rule or regulation shall cease to be entitled to the benefits of the Act.

We now come to a review of the labor provisions of the statute.

Section 7 (a) makes this statute the most important piece of labor legislation ever enacted in America. By this section employees are given the right to organize and bargain collectively through representatives of their own choosing. Collective bargaining is thus made a matter of definite federal law and compulsory on the management of all industry. The statute provides that this right of the workers to organize and bargain collectively through representatives of their own free choice shall be free from the interference, restraint or coercion of employers. Unrestricted free selection of labor representatives for collective bargaining is safeguarded by the statute and any interference by employers is a violation of law.

No employee and no one seeking employment shall be required as a condition of employment to join any company union or to refrain from joining, organizing, or assisting a labor organization of his own choosing.

These, very briefly, are the specifications of the Recovery Act in the interest of labor. Their construction and application in the past year have been an epoch in our economic history. Later chapters of this book will deal with the construction and constitutionality of these labor provisions.

Section 7 (b) provides that the President, so far as practicable, shall afford every opportunity to employers or employees in any trade or industry to establish by mutual agreement the standards as to the maximum hours of labor, minimum rates of pay, and such other conditions of employment as may be necessary in such trade or industry. The standards established in such agreements, when approved by the President, shall have the same effect as an approved code of fair competition.

Section 7 (c) reads that where no mutual agreement has been approved by the President, he may investigate the labor practices, policies, wages, hours of labor and conditions of employment in the trade or industry, and upon the basis of such investigation and after such hearings as he finds advisable, the President is authorized to prescribe a limited code of fair competition. Such a code shall fix maximum hours of labor, minimum rates of pay and other conditions of employment in the trade or industry as the President finds necessary to effectuate the law. Such limited codes of fair competition shall have the same effect as codes approved under the previous sections of the Act.

It is clear then that under Section 7 (c) the President may on his own motion, but after hearing, prescribe the wages, hours of labor and other conditions of employment in any trade or industry. What he prescribes has the effect of law.

National planning for trade and industry is contemplated by the Act. The President is granted power to establish an "industrial planning and research agency" to aid in carrying out his functions. Obviously, the power thus granted could be expanded to a vast practical operation. The powers and functions of the industrial planning and research agency are within the authority of the President to designate.

Section 7 (d) deals with the territorial scope of the Act. It applies to: (1) commerce between the States; (2) commerce between the States and foreign nations;

(3) commerce between the District of Columbia, or any Territory of the United States, any State, Territory or foreign nation; (4) between any insular possessions or other places under the jurisdiction of the United States; (5) between any such possessions or places and any State or Territory of the United States, or the District of Columbia, or any foreign nation; (6) or within the District of Columbia, or any Territory, or any insular possession or other place under the jurisdiction of the United States.

With respect to the scope of the law it should be noted that while by Section 3 it is addressed to all trade and industry and every subdivision thereof, the law is in fact limited in its operation by other concurrently effective statutes. It has no application to railroads which operate under other regulatory laws. It has no application to farmers whose activities are within the control and regulation of the AAA. Its application to banks is probably limited by other statutes. Over the functions of national banks Congress has special powers under the Constitution. (Art. I, Sec. 8, Par. Fifth.) With these exceptions, the statute operates with respect to all trade and industry and all transactions in trade and industry in or affecting interstate or foreign commerce. [Section 3, paragraph (b); Section 4, paragraph (b).]

The statute contains the express provision that nothing in the Act, or any regulation thereunder, shall prevent an individual from pursuing the vocation of manual labor and selling or trading the products thereof; nor shall anything in the Act, or regulation thereunder, prevent anyone from marketing or trading the produce of his farm. [Sec. 5 (a).]

Later provisions of the Act deal with the reconciliation of conflicts between the National Industrial Recovery Act and the Agricultural Adjustment Act and with special provisions affecting the oil industry. Under these sections all powers of the President under the agricultural statute may be delegated to the Secretary of Agriculture. With respect to the oil industry the President is authorized to prohibit the transportation in interstate and foreign commerce of petroleum produced or withdrawn from storage in excess of the amount permitted to be produced or withdrawn by any state law or valid regulation or order prescribed thereunder, by any board, commission, officer, or other duly authorized agency of a state. Any violation of any order of the President issued under the provisions of this subsection shall be punishable by a fine of not to exceed $1,000, or imprisonment for not to exceed six months, or both.

The final section is an extraordinary grant of power to the President. He is authorized to prescribe such rules and regulations as may be necessary to carry out the purposes of the Act. A violation of any such rule or regulation shall be punishable by fine of not to exceed $500, or imprisonment for not to exceed six months, or both. The President may from time to time cancel or modify any order, approval, license, rule, or regulation issued by him; and agreements, codes and licenses must contain an express provision to that effect. Under this broad grant of uncontrolled discretionary powers the President may prescribe such rules and regulations as he may deem necessary "to carry out the purposes of this title," and the violation of any such rule or regulation is punishable by fine or imprisonment. Without restriction these powers may be delegated.

I have now offered a digest of the essential provisions of the Recovery Act. The Act gives the President extraordinary powers but it requires of him practically no action. He is not required to approve or promulgate any code or any agreement, or grant any license, or prescribe any rule or regulation. Primarily and essentially the statute is legislation vesting extraordinary functions and powers in the President to meet the emergency, the exercise of which rests in his discretion. The intent of the law, however, is to bring all trade and industry under codes, because without codes the statute is lifeless. Undoubtedly a large degree of coöperation by government and industry and a wide measure of self-government by industry under codes are within the legislative scheme, but over this coöperation and self-government, or qualified self-government, rules the supreme power of the Administrator derived from the President. Provisions of all codes recognize this power.

Under this statute, the great experiment in federal industrial legislation, the NRA, will continue to function until June 16, 1935, unless sooner dissolved by the President or by the Congress. The Congress may also, of course, by an amendment to the law, extend the period of its operation. The Supreme Court may abruptly end it all by holding that in enacting the law the Congress transcended its power.

CHAPTER II

THE NATIONAL RECOVERY ADMINISTRATION

HAVING dwelt at length upon the nature and various sections of the Recovery Act, we now pass to a review of what has been done in its practical application. Our first task will be to describe the NRA as it rose to its present dimensions and power. The Act itself supplied the basis for the necessary procedure by vesting the President with the power to create all agencies necessary to fulfill the purposes of the law and to delegate to them any of his functions and powers. Under this broad grant of authority the problem before the President was the creation of an administrative organization for the making of codes for trade and industry. It was necessary that this organization be prepared and competent to cope with all the problems that would arise in the formation and administration of codes. No precedent existed in the experience of the government for the organization of the character required. The NRA is distinctly and completely a new administrative bureau. It is a marvelous fabric composed of a multitude of functioning units, with advisory and consultative divisions, all coördinated and interrelated, with defined jurisdictions and variegated duties and powers.

The formation of the NRA was accomplished with a rapidity that startled the country. The statute had the force of law on June 16, 1933. Immediately action began. The day the President affixed his signature to the Act he issued his Executive Order appointing an Administrator for Industrial Recovery under Title I of the

Act and constituting a Special Industrial Recovery Board composed of:

The Secretary of Commerce
The Attorney General
The Secretary of Agriculture
The Secretary of Labor
The Director of the Budget
The Administrator for Industrial Recovery
The Chairman of the Federal Trade Commission

Authority was vested in the Administrator subject to the general approval of the Special Industrial Advisory Board to select the necessary personnel on a temporary basis.

On June 19, 1933, only three days after the law became effective, the NRA issued an elaborate bulletin addressed to all trade associations and industrial and trade groups informing them that it was prepared to receive proposed codes and to conduct prompt hearings. It outlined the procedure necessary in the submission and formation of codes and recited many mandatory clauses for incorporation in all codes.

By a second Executive Order issued July 15, 1933, the Administrator, with the approval of the Special Industrial Recovery Board, was authorized to appoint the necessary personnel on a permanent basis, to fix their compensation, to conduct hearings, and to exercise such other functions as were vested in the President by Title I of the Act, with certain definite reservations of power to the President, which included, among others, the approval of codes, the making of agreements, the issuance of licenses and the exercise of the powers with respect to imports.

By a third Executive Order, the President vested the Administrator with power to approve of codes of fair competition, with the exception of codes for the major industries, and vested in the Administrator the approval of any changes in such codes. The major industries were classified as those normally employing in excess of 50,000 workers.

Upon the basis of these orders of the President, the organization of the NRA has been erected, with General Hugh S. Johnson as its architect and chief, with the title of Administrator. Immediately under General Johnson are his personal staff, the key functionaries of the Administration, consisting of the Assistant Administrator for Industry, Assistant Administrator for Labor, Assistant to the Administrator, Administrative Officer, Review Officer, Special Assistant Administrator, Assistant Administrator for Policy, General Counsel, Economic Adviser, Publicity Adviser, and Director of Enforcement. There is also an Executive Officer for the Administrator who coördinates all administrative functions and who has direct charge of a number of subsidiary divisions which serve all other units such as the Personnel Division, Control Division, Files and Mailing Sections.

Four important boards head the organization under the Administrator. They are the Industrial Advisory Board, which advises the Administrator on all matters affecting industry, the Labor Advisory Board, which advises the Administrator on all matters affecting labor, the Consumers Advisory Board, which advises the Administrator on all matters affecting the consumer, and the National Compliance Board, which hears cases of violations of codes and makes its recommendations to the Administration for action. The Industrial Advisory Board has a rotating membership so that, to use the official language, "fresh blood would constantly flow from industry to government and back to industry again, carrying knowledge and experience in a constant circulation."[1]

Another unit is known as the NRA Policy Board. This is an internal organization set up to advise the Administrator on all matters of general policy. The Administrator is chairman, the Executive Officer is vice-chairman and executive secretary. The members are the Assistant Administrators for Industry and Labor, Division Administrators, Chiefs of Divisions and the three Chairmen of the Industrial, Labor and Consumers Advisory Boards. There are also three sub-committees of this Board: Committee on Expedition of the Codes, Coördination Committee (to coördinate the administration of the approved codes), and the Code Authority Organization Committee.

A sixth and important unit, under the style of Code Authority Organization Committee, performs the functions of submitting to the Administrator proposed model administrative provisions for future codes, analyzes administrative provisions in existing codes, and, wherever necessary, submits proposed modifications. It considers and advises on plans proposed for code authority and trade association organizations for industrial self-government. It assists in effecting the organization of industries for code administration, and advises on the problems of coördinating the plans of industry for code administration with those of the NRA. Functioning with this Committee is a Trade Association Division which prepares plans for the organization of industry for industrial self-government.

The formation and approval of codes proceeds under an elaborate divisional organization. These divisions are the front line trenches of the NRA. Numerically

[1] NRA Release No. 1753.

designated are eight divisions now completely organized and in action. Each division is a unit in itself with legal advisers, technical experts and industrial, labor and consumer advisers. All of the industries of the country have been divided into groups and assigned to the various divisions. Each of these divisions supervises the preparation and administration of codes for the industries allocated to its jurisdiction.

Divisions, unnumbered, but having clearly defined jurisdiction, are Compliance, Public Relations, Legal, Review, Research and Planning, Imports, State Directors of Compliance, and Local Compliance Boards.

In the eight numbered divisions the major officials are Deputy Administrators who conduct hearings and do the actual work in the negotiation and completion of codes. They are the potent ministers of the NRA who deal direct with the representatives of trade and industry. At present there are fifteen of these Deputy Administrators. The Assistant Deputy Administrators are legion.

The Research and Planning Division is an active unit in the organization. It has the dual function of providing Deputy Administrators with impartial information and statistics which will aid them in determining if particular provisions of a code are fair, and of maintaining a group of expert economists who are relating the codes of various industries to one another. Their object is to foresee as far as possible the effect of each code on the industry itself and to insure the proper relationship and balance between various industries.[2]

The Import Division has been set up to make investigations preliminary to the exercise by the President of

[2] NRA Release No. 181 — August 4, 1933.

his power to restrict or cancel imports if necessary to effectuate the purposes of the Act.

By Executive Order of July 17, 1933, the President established a Central Statistical Board "to formulate standards for and to effect coördination of the statistical services of the Federal Government incident to the purposes of" the Recovery Act. The Board is empowered "to appraise and advise upon all schedules of all government agencies engaged in the primary collection of statistics required in carrying out the purposes of the National Industrial Recovery Act, to review plans for tabulation and classification of such statistics, and to promote the coördination and improvement of the statistical services involved." The board is composed partly of designated members and partly of members elected by the designated members. Members have been designated by the President, the Secretary of the Interior, the Secretary of Agriculture, the Secretary of Commerce, the Secretary of Labor, the Governor of the Federal Reserve Board, the Administrator for National Recovery and the Committee on Government Statistics and Information Services. The representative of the Recovery Administration on the board is the chief of its Research and Planning Division.

On November 17, 1933, the Special Industrial Recovery Board, appointed by the President on the day the Act became effective, was succeeded by the National Emergency Council. This body was created for the purpose of consolidating, coördinating and making more efficient and productive the emergency activities of the government and for the purpose of assisting and carrying into effect the provisions of the various emergency measures. Composing the National Emergency Council are the following:

The Secretary of the Interior (Administrator of Public Works)
The Secretary of Agriculture
The Secretary of Commerce
The Secretary of Labor
The Administrator of Agricultural Adjustment
The Administrator of Federal Emergency Relief
The Administrator for Industrial Recovery
The Chairman of the Home Owners' Loan Corporation
The Governor of the Farm Credit Administration
A Representative of the Consumers' Council

Now in energetic action in the administration of codes are the Code Authorities, new tribunals of great power, functioning under the supervision and subject to the approval of the Administrator. On these Code Authorities are administration members who are "co-workers in an understanding of public interest, concerned only in the faithful administration of the codes."[3] On May 20, 1934, it was announced that there were over 450 national codes and an equal number in process of formation. The whole trade and industry of the country is permeated with the orders and decrees of code authorities, national, regional and local, operating under these codes. The Code Authority is charged with the responsibility of administering the code. This requires the setting up of machinery for carrying out the trade practice provisions of the code, such prohibitions of unfair methods of competition, necessary cost accounting system, provisions against selling below cost, the open price policy, and all other practices that have been written into the codes. The Code Authority has the responsibility of policing the industry to prevent violations of the codes and the consideration and decision of complaints of the violations of trade practices.

[3] NRA Release No. 2251 — December 13, 1933.

Dictated alike by necessity and wisdom a process of decentralization of authority in detailed administration is going on under the NRA. In all the states of the Union there are state directors having various functions in connection with the administration and enforcement of codes. Regional compliance agencies, with their staffs of field workers, are scattered throughout the country. The state directors and these subordinate compliance agencies all function under the direction of the National Compliance Board at Washington. On January 31, 1934, the state officers held their first conference in Washington, and received general instructions on various phases of the relief and recovery program. They were charged within their respective jurisdictions with the administration of code compliance as their first official assignment.

Tied in with this vast organization are the National Labor Board and the Consumers Division of the National Emergency Council, actively functioning in dealing with strikes and labor disputes arising out of codes or their operation, in studying the effect of codes upon the small dealer and manufacturer, and the gathering in of complaints against undue price increases which at the moment are giving NRA officials deep concern.

The National Labor Board has established agencies in various parts of the country, known as Regional Labor Boards, for the settlement of disputes between employers and employees; and from the decisions of these subordinate agencies appeals may be taken to the central board.

On March 30, 1934, the Administrator issued an order for the creation of Industrial Relations Committees. All industries operating under approved codes which specifically provide for the creation of agencies for the adjustment of individual labor complaints and labor disputes are commanded to set up immediately such agencies. Industries operating under approved codes which do not specifically provide for the creation of agencies to handle labor disputes and complaints were requested immediately to proceed in each case to create an Industrial Relations Committee to handle both labor complaints and disputes. Procedure and standards were announced in an NRA Bulletin issued on March 30, 1934. The personnel, scope and functioning of these committees are subject to the approval of the Administrator.

This organization of boards, divisions, units and agencies, gigantic in proportions and still expanding, is staffed with an army, over 2,300 in all, of secretaries, assistants, clerks, lawyers, economists, accountants, stenographers, investigators, research workers, and other functionaries without number—all inspired by a zeal for public service; as busy a group of men and women as can be found in all the land. Rugged individualism lies far from the economics of the NRA but in its personnel are many rugged individuals. The members of the whole organization seem imbued with an enthusiasm and belief in the worthiness of the enterprise in which they are engaged, a pervasive feeling that the government is now doing something real and for the actual benefit of the nation.

Supplementing the NRA is the Federal Trade Commission, which under the statute may be required by the President to make such investigations as may be necessary to enable him to carry out the provisions of the Act, and also all United States District Attorneys in the country who are charged with the duty in their respective districts, under the direction of the Attorney General, to institute proceedings in equity to prevent and restrain violations of codes. On April 11, 1934, all District Attorneys were officially summoned into action to coöperate with the NRA Director of Enforcement or State Directors of Compliance in the adjustment of disputes under codes and for the institution and conduct of proceedings for the enforcement of codes.[4]

Now added to this vast federal organization are state and local officials of the states in which the model state recovery law prepared by the NRA has been adopted. This coöperation was intended by Congress as indicated by Section 2 (a) of the Act. The model law permits the governor of each state to consent to the utilization of state and local officers by the President in the enforcement of the NIRA. In the 23 states in which this law has been enacted the entire executive and administrative organization of the state may be invoked and utilized by the NRA, with the approval of the governor, for the enforcement of codes.

One more board, and that not an unimportant one, must have a place before we are done with this chapter. For an official inquiry into the activities of his organization the Administrator on February 9, 1934, announced a commission of inquiry. It is known as the Review Advisory Board and is designed to observe the effect of NRA codes upon all small enterprises. The Board is composed of six members. The Administrator assigned to this new Board adequate legal, research and clerical assistance for investigation of complaints made by small concerns that they are subject to undue hardships by the operation of codes.[5] This is the now famous Darrow Commission.

Supreme in authority over this whole organization is

[4] Department of Justice Release — April 11, 1934.
[5] Release No. 3371 — February, 1934.

the President. The NRA is his direct creation. All power emanates from him and his approval, direct or indirect, is essential to the operation of all regulations and codes. His position is not nominal but one of active and arduous responsibility. It requires the unfailing insight of a great realist. The President must preserve balance and proportion. He must weigh the deeper significance of every policy. One critical situation follows another requiring his decision and action.

"Wisdom lies
In the masterful administration of the unforseen."

The purpose of this colossal machine of government is the regulation and control and moral renovation of trade and industry under codes of fair competition. The formation, approval, promulgation and enforcement of codes have engaged the major efforts of the NRA. This power and authority and these manifold and momentous activities proceed upon the legal foundation of Section 3 (a) of the statute providing for the formation of "a code or codes of fair competition for the trade or industry or subdivision thereof."

CHAPTER III

THE PROCESS OF CODE-MAKING AND ITS RESULTS

WITH the NRA in action the process of code-making rapidly developed. The administration of the Recovery Act did not in truth wait upon its adoption, but actively preceded it. This was true to such a degree that on the day the President signed the measure he was able to announce to the country the appointment of the Administrator and a Special Industrial Recovery Board and that "this organization is now prepared to receive proposed codes and to conduct prompt hearings looking toward their submission to me for approval."[1] Three days after the law became effective the Bulletin of the NRA, to which I have before alluded, admonished all trade associations and industrial and labor groups to proceed with the submission of codes. Procedure was definitely outlined and many important provisions for all codes were proposed. The first code approved and signed was that for the Cotton Textile Industry. This truly historic event occurred on July 9, 1933.

The initial procedure in code-making is the drafting of a proposed code by a trade or industrial association representing the trade or industry for submission to the NRA. "It is not the function of the National Recovery Administration to prescribe what shall be in the codes to be submitted by associations or groups. The initiative in all such matters is expected to come from within the industry itself."[2] The code is then assigned to a unit of the NRA over which a deputy administrator presides.

[1] Appendix III.
[2] NRA Bulletin No. 2, p. 2.

It is examined, its provisions carefully analyzed and revised according to the views of the NRA and, in most instances, entirely rewritten. It is then set down for a public hearing. These public hearings are constantly and concurrently proceeding with respect to many trades and industries. The following excerpt from a Washington newspaper in May, 1934, suggests the almost feverish activity of the NRA in the formation of codes:

TODAY
CODE HEARINGS

9:30 A.M. — Folding Box Authority. Mayflower Hotel
10 A.M. — Motion Picture Laboratories. Willard Hotel
10 A.M. — Fly Swatter Manufacturing Industry. Willard Hotel
10 A.M. — Mil and Dress Trim, Braid and Tex. Willard Hotel
10 A.M. — Men's Neckwear. Raleigh Hotel
10 A.M. — Pipe Tool Mfg. Raleigh Hotel
10 A.M. — Vise Mfg. Raleigh Hotel
10 A.M. — Whlse. Cop., Brass, Bronze and Rel. Al. Carlton Hotel
10 A.M. — Button Jobbers' Trade. Washington Hotel
10 A.M. — Machinery and Allied Prod. Carlton Hotel
10 A.M. — Gas Powered Industrial Truck. Carlton Hotel
10 A.M. — Pulp and Paper Machinery. Carlton Hotel
10 A.M. — Multiple-V Belt Drive. Carlton Hotel
10 A.M. — Mechanical Press Mfg. Carlton Hotel

The procedure in connection with all these hearings is substantially the same. Representatives of the trade or industrial association, generally acting through a committee, accompanied by legal counsel, appear in Washington in response to the notice for the hearing. On the day preceding the public hearing representatives of the NRA meet the code committee and its counsel for an informal conference known in the NRA as a "dress rehearsal." This conference is attended by the Deputy Administrator, or one of his important assistants, and by representatives of the Law, Industrial, Labor, Consumers, and Planning and Research Divisions. These representatives of the specialized agencies of the Recovery Administration are there to aid and advise the Chairman in the consideration of the various provisions of the code. During this informal round table conference efforts are made to reconcile the conflicting views of the proponents of the code and the NRA. The conditions and needs of the trade or industry about to be codified are fully discussed, the points of view of the industry and of the various agencies of the NRA are made known, and the ground is laid for the public hearing on the succeeding day. All agreements reached at this informal hearing are embodied in amendments to the proposed code.

The public hearing on the following day is more formal. It is presided over by a Deputy Administrator, and at the table with him sit representatives of the Labor, Advisory, Consumers, Law and Planning and Research Divisions. Attending the hearing are many members of the industry, manufacturers and dealers, and representatives of public, consumer and labor organizations. Labor organizations are seeking just and fair provisions for labor. Manufacturers are seeking just and fair provisions for the stockholders and management. The NRA legal adviser is there to see that the code in no way conflicts with the statutes and embodies all the mandatory provisions of the law. Consumer representatives are present to see that the public is protected against monopoly, and that prices do not rise out of proportion to the increased cost under codes, and that trade and marketing practices are not injurious to the public. As the hearing is in the true sense public anyone who registers is entitled to express his views and convictions. The Deputy Administrator is the master of ceremonies. All witnesses who desire to be heard are interrogated by him. Each provision of the code is read and discussed and all objections heard and entered of record. Sharply conflicting points of view appear. Heated arguments and emotional appeals are not uncommon. The hearings are intensely interesting and at times dramatic.

Upon the conclusion of the public hearing, the formation of the code is taken under advisement by the NRA, but before final action is taken post-hearings, so-called, are held between the officials of the NRA and the representatives of the industry. These hearings are not public, but are informal conferences around a table. At this stage the procedure in the formation of a code somewhat resembles the ancient rite of trial by battle. Controverted issues are definitely drawn. Conflicts of views, purposes and arguments between the functionaries of the NRA and the representatives of the industry develop. Representatives of the industry naturally take the point of view dictated by its interests and needs. The point of view of the NRA is naturally the public interest, or what is conceived to be the public interest. Various groups of producers or dealers may differ as to the needs of the industry. Geographical sections may be aligned against each other. Officials within the NRA may have conflicting views. The conferences, or post-hearings, go on, and in many instances are greatly prolonged, until the provisions of the code are finally worked out, and when worked out they are usually the embodiment of a series of compromises. Edmund Burke declared that all government is founded on compromise and barter. This is particularly true of government under industrial codes.

The questions that delay the formation and approval

of codes deal with a great variety of matters. The maximum working hours to be prescribed for a trade or industry is one of the most troublesome problems. As customs and conditions in the industries are extremely variant, it is not possible to fix one rule or standard. What is fair and practicable in one business may be wholly unfair and unsuited to another. Likewise, the question of minimum wages is a constant subject for controversy and argument. Unfair trade practices to be prohibited, the constitution of the Code Authority, the definition of the industry to be brought within the code, are all matters that must be carefully considered and settled in accordance with the facts and conditions of each trade and industry.

Procedure in code-making goes on under a barrage of executive, administrative and office orders. A proposed provision for a code which may be mandatory in the morning may be optional in the afternoon. Standard provisions are being constantly reworded. Entirely new provisions are devised and proposed from day to day. Decisions for a particular code made during one hearing may be reversed at a later conference. Policies mastered by events change overnight. Orders from above are constantly directing the movements and determining the decisions of those at work in the negotiation and completion of the codes. The office of General Johnson is the mount from which thunder forth the new commandments.

The position of the Deputy Administrator in charge of the procedure for the formation of a code is one of strategic importance. He must combine the qualities of a diplomat and statesman and, it may be added, an athlete. He must have frame and punch. His work requires a high degree of physical vitality and endurance.

In his own organization divergent and conflicting views develop among the Industrial Advisory Board, Labor, Law, Consumers and Planning Divisions, which he must reconcile. Each of these divisions may propose provisions for a code contrary to his sound judgment, which provisions he must tactfully eliminate. Serious difficulties are often encountered in the NRA itself in making the final adjustments.

The first requisite for the successful regulation of industry is understanding. The second is a keen sense of justice. The third is a balanced judgment. The greatest hindrance is a keen and dominant sense of authority. The views of men who are actually running a business and of those seeking to impose rules upon it will, no doubt, always radically and honestly differ. "Men's judgments are parcels of their fortunes."

During all these proceedings the word "stockholder" is seldom heard. The appearance of a committee of stockholders at a code conference would be quite a shock and probably an unwelcome intrusion. In every step taken, however, by the NRA the interests of stockholders are vitally concerned. The formation of a code of regulations for a business to which operations cannot be adjusted with success is the essence of folly. Essential to our economic system are reasonable profits to manufacturers. Factories cannot continue to operate and produce the goods the nation needs without an adequate supply of capital, and capital will abandon any industry in which it is not assured of fair profits. Fair profits are equally essential for the security of labor. The primary interest of all is to keep the industry supplied with adequate capital for continuous normal operation. These interests are all bound together in the vision of President Roosevelt. "Its goal" [NRA], he declared, "is the assurance of a reasonable profit to industry and living wages for labor with the elimination of the piratical methods and practices which have not only harassed honest business but also contributed to the ills of labor."[3]

The ideal code will have many essential features. It will be in complete compliance with the statute, apply to the conditions in the industry which it seeks to regulate, be practical, work no unnecessary hardship or injustice; all its provisions will function harmoniously, and in its actual operation it will be fair and equitable to the consuming public, labor, management and stockholders.

After all the procedure we have described, the proposed code, if it is one for a major industry, is submitted to the President by the Administrator. If the President finds that the Code is in compliance with the statute, contains all the requisites which the statute prescribes, and will tend to effectuate the declared purposes of the Act, it receives his approval and signature, and the code-making process is complete. With relation to codes for the minor industries, the final action of approval or disapproval is within the power of the Administrator.

After a code has been approved an application for a stay of its operation may be made by one who did not participate in establishing or consenting to the code. This procedure is authorized by Executive Order 6205-B of July 15, 1933. Under this order any code of fair competition approved by the President shall be deemed in full force and effect on the effective date as stated in the code; but after the approval of a code, hearings may be given by the Administrator or his designated representative to persons who have not in person or by a representative participated in establishing or consenting to

[3] See *On Our Way,* by Franklin D. Roosevelt (1933), page 97. John Day Co.

a code, but who are directly affected. Those who claim that the application of the code in particular instances is unjust to them may apply for an exception to, or exemption from, or modification of the code. Such persons applying, within ten days, shall be given an opportunity for a hearing and determination of the issues raised, prior to incurring any liability through enforcement of the code, and if justice requires, the Administrator shall stay the application of the code to all similarly affected, pending a determination of the issues raised.

Certain provisions are mandatory and must be included in all codes:

The statutory labor provisions. The language of the statute must be incorporated in the code;

A clause to meet the requirements of Section 10 (b) of the Act relative to modification by the President;

Express provisions that the code shall not permit monopolies or monopolistic practices.

Certain conditions are attached to all codes. The President is authorized to approve a code only if he finds the following:

That the association or group admits equitably to membership all who are engaged in the same trade or industry;

That the association or group is truly representative of the trade or industry for which it speaks;

That the code presented will not promote a monopoly;

That the code will not oppress or discriminate against small enterprises;

That employees will have the right to organize and bargain collectively, through representatives of their own choosing;

That no employee will be required as a condition of employment to sign an anti-union or so-called "yellow dog" contract;

That employers will comply with the maximum hours of labor and minimum rates of pay and standards for other working conditions approved by the President;

That the code will tend to effectuate the policy of this title.

Provisions of the codes cover a wide range of trade and industrial activities. Maximum working hours in the trade or industry are prescribed and also whatever exceptions to basic working hours are deemed necessary. Separate provisions as to working hours are usually made for factory and office employees. In many codes an averaging of working time is allowed over a definite period, say six months, subject to specified maximum working hours per day. Provisions fixing working time have been the subject of much contest between various industries and the NRA. It is by and through provisions of codes that the NRA seeks to solve the stupendous problem of unemployment. According to its official figures the labor policies of the NRA have placed 3,000,000 unemployed back at work.

Minimum hourly wages are prescribed in the codes. In some codes there are differentials in minimum wages according to population of the cities in which the plants are located. Factory employees and office employees are usually dealt with separately, and in many codes there is a differential in fixing minimum wages as between men and women, and in some few codes a differential between male employees under 21 and over 21 years of age. As a rule, codes contain the provisions that female employees performing substantially the same work as male employees shall receive the same rates of pay. Coupled with the provisions fixing minimum wages is a clause dealing with equitable adjustment of wages above the minimum. This is usually a declaration that members of the industry shall endeavor to increase the pay of all employees in excess of the minimum wages, as set forth in the code, by an equitable adjustment of all pay schedules. Special wage provisions are made for learners, apprentices and infirm employees. Coupled with all these wage provisions, and the provisions covering maximum hours, are the mandatory labor provisions specified in the statute.

NRA codes have abolished child labor and eliminated the sweatshop. No greater achievement for human welfare is recorded in our history. The only possible exception to this statement may be the emancipation of the negro from slavery. One was a victory of war, and the other, no less renowned, of peace. In all codes the minimum age of employment is 16 years. Usually there is also a provision that no person under 18 can be attached to a hazardous occupation.

Important provisions of approved codes deal with prices. In many codes the open price system is established by the code. Under such a plan each member of the industry files with the Code Authority a list showing the prices, with terms and discounts applicable thereto, for all his products sold to the regular trade, and the code requires that there shall be no deviation from the prices, terms and discounts as thus filed until revisions of the schedules have been duly put into effect in accordance with the code. With few exceptions the codes require that revisions of price schedules must be filed and published for a prescribed period of time before they can become effective. A ten-day waiting period is usually specified. The purpose of these provisions is to prevent the concealment of price-cutting from competitors; to prevent the enticing of customers with special bargaining; to prevent the cutting below a self-imposed standard price while nominally maintaining it. They seek to prevent evasions of restrictions on price-cutting. The open price system supplies the indispensable requirement for price control. Obviously its administration and enforcement is a task of great difficulty. The test of its efficacy is whether or not it can be enforced against dissenters and chiselers resorting to evasions.

Another usual and important provision dealing with prices is the prohibition of sales below the individual cost of production. Prohibition against selling an article below its cost of production constitutes the most common price-controlling device in the approved codes.

Incorporated in most of the codes is a list of unfair trade practices which are prohibited. One of the cardinal objectives of the National Recovery Act stated in its definition of policy is "to eliminate unfair competitive practices." Trades and industries must be dealt with separately, in accordance with their own conditions and needs in framing these unfair trade practices to the end that unfair competition and all practices in the trade or industry that smack of deception, trickery or dishonesty will be extirpated, and fair competitive dealing in the merchandising of the products of the industry will be assured. These code provisions are a canon of ethics for business. They are more than pious declarations; they are regulations which by incorporation in the code are given the force of law.

Unfair trade rules deal with a great variety of practices including those which tend to aid or conceal fraud, false accounting, false invoicing, inaccurate advertising, inaccurate labeling, pre-dating and post-dating of invoices, secret or concealed rebates, fictitious bidding to mislead competitors, infringements, style piracy, and discrimination among customers of the same class.

Many of these unfair trade practices, now incorporated in the codes and made illegal, have often been denounced by the Federal Trade Commission in its decisions, such as commercial bribery, gratuities or rebates to any purchaser, prospective purchaser or dealer, hidden concessions in prices, and discrimination against certain customers or classes of customers.

Provisions of many codes deal with production control schemes. These are of three types, providing either for the allocation of production by the allotment of production quotas to individual members of the industry, or by limiting total production, or by preventing the expansion of plant or production facilities without the consent of the Administrator.

Limitations of working hours necessarily affect production. Provisions for the limitation of new capacity appear in a considerable number of approved codes and in a variety of forms. In certain codes arrangements are embodied prohibiting any member of the industry from expanding his present productive capacity without first obtaining the consent of the Administrator.

In framing all the provisions of codes two of the most difficult problems before the NRA are the protection of the small merchant and manufacturer and the protection of the consuming public. Codes should be framed so that the small unit in the industry can comply with their terms and survive. In arrangements for price stabilization and control of production the interests of the consuming public must be considered and guarded. I can only allude to these problems here, but they are fundamental and are inherent in any national plan of regulation of trade and industry.

Provisions also exist in many codes for economic planning in the industry. This, as we have seen, is another important objective of the Recovery Act.

Of paramount importance are provisions of the codes

dealing with the constitution of the Code Authority. Through the Code Authority the trade or industry is organized for self-government under federal supervision.

Primarily the jurisdiction to administer and enforce a code is vested in the Code Authority. A Code Authority coöperates with the Administrator in the administration of the code. The Code Authority can be likened to a court of original jurisdiction, with the Administrator as the court of appeal.

Provisions differ in the various codes as to the constitution and power of the Code Authority. A typical set-up of a Code Authority found in many codes consists of five individuals selected by members of the industry and three additional members without vote to represent the Administrator. The selection of the five individuals constituting the Code Authority is made under a formula for voting by members of the industry, based on the amount of annual dollar sales. It has been accepted by the NRA that voting based upon the volume of business is the best method of giving just representation to every member of the industry. The administration members of the code authorities represent the government and the public interest in the faithful administration of the codes.[4]

In numerous codes there are Regional Code Authorities and in some instances a further delegation of functions to some sort of a local authority.

The Code Authority is the supervisory and planning agency for the industry, subject to the limitations that many of its acts require the approval of the Administrator. "The extent to which the Code Authority," declares an official statement of the NRA, "will formulate plans for the stabilization and prosperity of its indus-

[4] NRA Release No. 2251 — December 13, 1933.

try depends entirely upon the wishes of the industry itself, and the degree of leadership to be found in the personnel of the Code Authority."[5]

Codes go into great detail in dealing with the powers and duties of the Code Authority. The objective of all these powers is to insure the execution of the provisions of the code and to provide for the compliance by all members of the industry with the provisions of the applicable code. Each Code Authority adopts its own bylaws and rules and regulations. Its power to require information from the members of the industry is broadly stated to embrace all information and reports as are required for the administration of the code. The Code Authority is usually vested with the power to use such trade associations and other agencies as it deems proper for the carrying out of any of its activities. It is also charged with the responsibility of making recommendations to the Administrator for the coördination of the administration of its code with such other codes as may be related to the industry.

Other duties usually imposed upon the Code Authority are to recommend to the Administrator any action or measures deemed advisable, including further fair trade practice provisions to govern members of the industry in their relations with one another or with other industries; measures for industrial planning, and stabilization of employment; and modification of the code, which shall become effective upon approval by the Administrator after such notice and hearing as he may specify.

Recent codes also provide for the appointment of two committees which in certain industries are important; one, a Trade Practice Committee, and the other an

[5] NRA Release No. 2251 — December 13, 1933.

Industrial Relations Committee. The duty of the Trade Practice Committee is to meet with similar committees appointed under such other codes as may be related to the industry for the purpose of formulating fair trade practices to govern the relationships between employers under its code and under such other codes to the end that such fair trade practices may be proposed to the Administrator as amendments to its code and other codes.

The Industrial Relations Committee has to do with the settlement of labor disputes. It consists of an equal number of representatives of employers and employees and an impartial chairman. The Administrator appoints such impartial chairman upon the failure of the Committee to select one by agreement. If no truly representative organization exists the employee members of such board may be nominated by the Labor Advisory Board of the NRA and appointed by the Administrator. The employer representatives are chosen by the Code Authority. The Committee deals with complaints and disputes relating to labor in accordance with rules and regulations issued by the Administrator. The Industrial Relations Committee may establish such Divisional, Regional and Local adjustment agencies as it may deem advisable, each of which shall be constituted in like manner as the Central Committee.

The atmosphere with respect to the disputed matter of expenses of code administration was recently clarified by an Executive Order and by an Administrative Order, simultaneously issued by the Administrator. The Executive Order is dated April 14, 1934, and it makes provision for clauses in codes relating to the collection of expenses of code administration and authorizes regulations governing such collections. The Executive Order provides that the code authority, subject to the approval of the Administrator, is authorized to incur reasonable obligations necessary and proper for the administration and enforcement of the code, and the funds collected shall be held in trust for the purposes of the code. It further provides that the budget of estimated expenses of the Code Authority shall be submitted to the Administrator and approved by him. This budget shall show the equitable basis upon which the funds necessary to support the budget shall be contributed by members of the industry.

Under the Administrative Order members of the industry may file a protest and have a hearing as to the fairness of the assessments made upon the basis of the budget.

The Executive Order and the Administrative Order both expressly provide that the failure to pay an assessment properly made in accordance with these orders is a violation of any code containing provisions for assessments for expenses.

There are certain definite legal points as to all codes. Three of them may be stated as follows:

A code must be in harmony with the National Industrial Recovery Act. Upon elementary principles any provision of a code which infringes upon the statute would be void.

A code approved by the President has the force of law and is in effect a criminal statute. Section 3 (b) of the statute expressly provides that after the President "shall have approved any such code, the provisions of such code shall be the standards of fair competition for such code or industry or subdivision thereof."

Codes are enforcible by injunction. Section 3 (c) of the Recovery Act vests in the District Courts of the United States the duty to prevent and restrain violations of any code of fair competition approved under the Act.

The modification of an existing code without a hearing and without the consent of the industry would appear to be unauthorized because a code is in the nature of a contract between the assenting members of the industry and the government of the United States. Every sound principle would require that before a change in an existing code could be made by the government there should be a hearing with the trade or industry and the change should be negotiated and agreed to.

Overlapping of codes has become a perplexing and difficult problem. The conflict often arises before the code is approved in connection with the definition of the trade or industry to be embraced within the operation of the code. Manufacturers operating under a particular code, who produce similar or related articles to those produced by an industry about to be placed under a code, will appear and endeavor to restrict the operation of the proposed code. These conflicts resemble trade union battles over jurisdiction, although probably less violent. It is of the utmost importance that a particular trade or industry, and the products and articles produced within that industry, be explicitly defined in the code so that its application or non-application to a particular manufacturer or dealer or particular product can be readily ascertained. The overlapping of codes with respect to various commodities is particularly difficult in its application to a company which produces in the same factory products embraced within two or more codes. Production is a unit and it is not possible to operate a plant with different working hours and different working conditions governed by various and conflicting codes. A large corporation manufacturing a great variety of products is now affected by 31 codes. Recently a procedure was announced by the NRA for the granting of exemptions from all codes excepting that code which applies to the largest volume of the production. A large mail order house in the Middle West is subject in its merchandising process to over 100 codes. This problem of the overlapping and conflicting application of codes is giving the NRA grave concern.

Cumulative experience is fast demonstrating that there must be a restriction of code-making. A concatenation of myriad code provisions now overspreads the country regulating with minutissimic detail and the rigidity of a criminal statute the occupations and trades and daily business of the people. All commercial and industrial activity in every nook and corner of the land, in every hamlet and neighborhood, is caught in this network of code regulations. It is a bewilderingly complex legalism that has settled upon the minor daily occupations and activities of men and women. Many strictly local enterprises, small neighborhood shops, barber shops, dyers and cleaners, local restaurants, beauty shops, and other commercial activities cannot successfully be drawn within the operation of codes. The work of the NRA must be confined to important industries amenable to national control or it will break down. Realities must be recognized and the line drawn between industries that can be embraced under a national organization and all their activities so governed and those that cannot be nationally regulated or controlled. Many objections to this withdrawal of the NRA will be urged but it must yield to the inexorable sway of events and realities. Facts are stubborn and regulation by government must be adjusted to conditions and not to theories if it is to be something more than form. The constitutional question I shall discuss later, but at this point I suggest that with regard to a business or occupation strictly and wholly local, not related to or affecting interstate or foreign commerce, factual basis for federal power is lacking.[6]

The importance of codes as legal and economic agencies cannot be overstressed. By certain major industries they are hailed as new charters of coöperation. They afford a wide field for concerted and coöperative action which hitherto has been held illegal. To industry they are a challenge to just and enlightened and effective self-government. They are a challenge to labor and management to work out harmonious relations in all industrial processes. The success and effectiveness of the government of industry by and under codes is the great experiment of the NRA. The legal conundrum of the century is the constitutionality of the statute under which the codes are in operation.

[6] Since this paragraph was written the elimination in part of code enforcement with respect to local service activities has been officially ordered by the NRA.

CHAPTER IV

THE APPLICATION OF THE LABOR PROVISIONS

IN A preceding chapter I stated that the Recovery Act is the most important piece of labor legislation ever enacted in this country. Other commentators have asserted that the whole Act is essentially a labor law. This sweeping characterization is hardly justified by the text of the Act. The objectives expressed in the preamble, of "promoting the organization of industry for the purpose of coöperative action in trade groups" and the elimination of "unfair competitive practices" and of "obstructions to the free flow of interstate and of foreign commerce," and the sections of the Act in the execution of these purposes, give the statute a wide measure of operation independent of the mandates with respect to labor. The labor clauses were intended to promote harmony and coöperation between labor and management. Their purpose was, in the language of Congress, "to induce and maintain *united action* of labor and management under adequate governmental sanction and supervision." History since June, 1933, has given the labor provisions transcendent importance.

In dealing with the application of the labor provisions of the Recovery Act we are entering the sector of industrial conflict. Here issues profoundly affect the economic structure and the social welfare. It is a field of warfare for advantage and ascendency and domination, of threats and intimidation and coercion, of force and violence, of picketing, strikes, lockouts and boycotts, of bombing and bloodshed and of racketeering. Conflicts between capital and labor will not be ended by statute.

Isolated judicial decisions will have little effect upon this mass of human conflict. The sense of justice, humane and enlightened attitudes, cool reason and calm judgment, the desire to understand and the clear understanding of facts and conditions must rule if greater coöperation and harmony are to prevail.

The President, in signing the Recovery Act, declared:

> "This law is also a challenge to labor. Workers, too, are here given a new charter of rights long sought and hitherto denied."[1]

The now famous Section 7 (a) is the charter of rights of labor to which the President refers. By that section the right of labor to bargain collectively and to act through representatives of its own selection, independently and freely chosen, is directly and unequivocally declared. The three declarations of Section 7 (a) are:

> (1) Employees shall have the right to organize and bargain collectively through representatives of their own choosing and shall be free from the interference, restraint, or coercion of employers of labor, or their agents, in the designation of such representatives or in self-organization or in other concerted activities for the purpose of collective bargaining or other mutual aid or protection.
>
> (2) No employee and no one seeking employment shall be required as a condition of employment to join any company union or to refrain from joining, organizing, or assisting a labor organization of his own choosing.
>
> (3) Employers shall comply with the maximum hours of labor, minimum rates of pay, and other conditions of employment, approved or prescribed by the President.

Reduced to simpler terms, Section 7 (a) assures to labor that:

[1] Bulletin of NRA No. 1 — June 16, 1933.

Employees have the right to organize into a group or groups.

These groups may select their own representatives to deal with the management in collective bargaining.

Discrimination against employees because of their labor affiliations is prohibited.

These affirmations written into the statute are mandatory for all codes. All codes contain their verbatim repetition. They must go into codes without any modification. As to this the law gives the administration no discretion. The provisions operate only under and through codes. Prior to the approval of a code the NRA has no jurisdiction to deal with disputes between employers and employees, or to compel employers to deal with any employee organization. The provisions of Section 7 (a), and all other provisions with respect to maximum hours, wages and working conditions, when incorporated in an approved code, are binding on labor as well as management. A strike intended to break down provisions of a code with respect to wages or hours or working conditions would be plainly in violation of the code. The rights and procedure established by Section 7 (a) apply, according to the plain wording of the statute, to all industry, local and interstate, operating under codes. They apply to every worker and every employer in America. The construction of these provisions is a matter not for the NRA but for the courts. The grave question as to the power of Congress to impose these mandates upon every employer of labor must meet the final test of judicial review.

Other provisions in the statute require that the President shall, so far as practicable, afford every opportunity to employers and employees to establish by mutual agreement the labor standards for the trade or industry. Such standards, when thus agreed upon and when approved by the President, are made binding on all employers within the industry. In the absence of such an approved mutual agreement, the President, after investigation, may prescribe and establish in a limited code of fair competition the maximum hours of labor, the minimum rates of pay, and other conditions of employment necessary to effectuate the purpose of the law. In thus acting the President "may differentiate according to experience and skill of the employees affected and according to the locality of employment; but no attempt shall be made to introduce any classification according to the nature of the work involved which might tend to set a maximum as well as a minimum wage."

Considering all of the labor provisions, it is clear that they confer upon organized labor vitally important prerogatives. Collective bargaining is made compulsory and a matter of law. Representatives of labor acting in collective bargaining are to be designated by the free and independent choice of labor, unhampered by "the interference, restraint or coercion of employers." Correlative obligations and duties are likewise imposed upon labor; the duty of coöperating with employers in endeavoring to reach mutual agreements and to maintain harmonious relations. Labor, enriched in its legal rights, is also by this statute placed within government regulation and control. Over all is the supreme power of the President explicitly declared in the Act.

Regarding the construction of Section 7 (a), controversy and strife are raging. Its reasonable interpretation does not appear a matter of insuperable difficulty.

It fixes the right of employees to organize, to bargain collectively, and to select their representatives for collective bargaining by their own free choice, and therefore, employees may join a labor union, or form a labor union, and deal with their employer through the officials of such union if they so choose.

Employees may also refrain from joining a labor union, and may deal with their employers through a selected number of their fellow employees, or they may deal with their employer individually.

Employees may legally form a company union, or may adopt a form of shop committee or employee representation plan, but the employer cannot legally interfere with or coerce his employees in the matter of selection of representatives or in self-organization.

On the other hand, employees who do not wish to join a labor union are given the right to deal with their employer through their own selected representatives. It would appear to be contrary to the plain intent of the statute that employees who do not wish to join a labor union should be interfered with or coerced by those seeking to force them into labor union membership. Employees, however, have the right to solicit their fellow employees to join a labor union and to have such labor union represent them in their collective bargaining with their employers.

A grave question arises as to the legality of a closed-shop agreement and similar agreements between a manufacturer and a union. The terms of Section 7 (a), assuring continuing freedom of action to all employees in choosing their representatives to deal with employers, would seem to invalidate an agreement of the management constituting any specific union as the selected spokesman of labor. A closed-shop contract, prohibiting employment of persons not members of a particular union, would discriminate against employees who were members of other unions, or of no organization at all. Such a contract would seem to be a definite interference with the employee's continuing freedom of choice contrary to the provisions of the Act.

The obligation of the employer to join in collective bargaining with his employees through representatives freely chosen is free from doubt, but it does not require either side to accept any specific demands. The Act does not go so far as to say that the employer and employees must achieve a bargain. It does not require them to enter into any agreement unless a fair agreement can be reached. But the statute plainly implies good faith and honest efforts by both labor and management.

The second declaration of Section 7 (a) is plain. It declares that "no employee and no one seeking employment shall be required as a condition of employment to join any company union or to refrain from joining, organizing, or assisting a labor organization of his own choosing."

Under this language it is clear that an employer cannot lawfully discharge an employee for the sole reason of membership in a labor union.

The so-called "merit clause" is now barred from all codes, but the relative merits of union and non-union workers are within the final judgment of the employer. This interpretation of Section 7 (a) was officially declared by President Roosevelt in a letter to General Johnson. The President stated:

"While there is nothing in the provisions of Section 7 (a) to interfere with the *bona fide* exercise of the right of an employer to select, retain, or advance employees on the basis of individual merit, Section 7 (a) does clearly prohibit the pretended exercise of this right by an employer simply as a device for compelling employees to refrain from exercising their right of self-organization, designation of representatives and collective bargaining, which are guaranteed to all employees in said Section 7 (a)."[2]

The merit clause is important in plants in which there is a vast variety of operations and a great difference in the individual merits of workmen. Where the jobs require long experience and skill the individual experience and capacity of the workmen must be considered if justice is to be done. In such plants the dealing with men and women on the basis of individual merit is an essential daily experience.

An employer is not required by law to hire any man, and for any reason an employer can refuse such employment, but it is unlawful for an employer to fix as a condition of employment that the man shall join any company union or shall refrain from joining, organizing or assisting a labor organization of his own choosing.

The third declaration of Section 7 (a) is the explicit mandate that employers shall comply with the maximum hours of labor, minimum rates of pay, and other conditions of employment approved or prescribed by the President.

Sharp and bitter controversy has arisen in the construction of Section 7 (a) with respect to collective bargaining by company unions and shop committees. Company unions and committees of workers are clearly legal if they are freely organized by the employees. Company unions or other groups organized through the "interference, restraint or coercion of employers" have no legal status in collective bargaining. The words "interference," "restraint," or "coercion," like all other language of statutes, must be reasonably applied. It refers to acts that are distinctly directing, restraining or coercive in

[2] *New York Times*, October 24, 1933, page 16.

nature. Interviews between labor and management, mutual counsel and advice, suggestions and statements of employers, would not *per se,* according to any reasonable construction, constitute a violation of the law. But the employees must be left completely free to accept or reject any suggestions or advice. Pressure in any form, by words or actions, direct or indirect, is against the spirit if not the letter of the statute. If company unions or other group representatives within the plant are to act in collective bargaining that decision must be the free and independent action of the employees whom they represent.

Employees have the right to solicit their fellow employees, peaceably and without coercion, to join a local union or a national union. They have no right to do this by using intimidation or coercion. Under all these conditions the importance of the meaning ultimately to be given by the courts to the words "intimidation," "coercion," "interference" in the construction of the Recovery Act is obvious.

The right of employees to affiliate with national unions and to have such unions represent them in collective bargaining is equally plain and indubitable. The statutory right to organize and to bargain collectively through representatives of their own choosing seems a clear legal foundation of the action of employees in affiliating individually or through local organizations with national unions and having the agents of such unions represent them in collective bargaining. Under the language of the Act the representatives need not be employees. The duty of employers to bargain with any representatives properly selected is ordained.

Recently Vice-Chancellor Fallon of the Court of

Errors and Appeals in New Jersey, in a case before him,[3] construed Section 7 (a) as a mandate of the law which "confers on employees the right to bargain collectively through representatives of their own choosing, which connotes the right to strike." "The right to strike," the court declared, "includes the right to use peaceable and lawful means to induce present employees and expectant employees to join the ranks." Under Section 7 (a), the court decided, employees have a right to form their own individual unions and to affiliate their own "individual unions with a body organized to promote the common aims and purposes." The precise question of the right to strike in order to break down an approved code was not involved in that case.

The point of greatest difficulty is the method of selection by employees of their representatives for collective bargaining. The statute does not prescribe the manner of selection. It simply confers the right to select representatives for collective bargaining. The exercise of this right must be free and unhampered either by employers, by national labor unions, or by other employees. The employees of any particular plant have a statutory right to their own free choice. The law does not provide that a majority of the employees can dictate to the minority. Under the law, any individual worker is free to join a company union, a national union, or any group or organization, or to deal for himself with the management. The language of the Act gives to each and every employee the right to select and bargain through representatives of his own choosing. Individual as well as collective freedom of action by employees is guarded and assured.

[3] *Bayonne Textile Corp.* v. *American Fed. of Silk Workers,* New Jersey Court of Errors and Appeals, Oct. 26, 1933.

It would seem a plain implication of the statute that a code when approved by the President, fixing maximum hours, minimum wages, and other conditions of employment, is, with respect to the conditions included within the code, binding upon the workers in the industry to which the code applies. The code has the force of law and as law it deals with certain specified labor relations and conditions. As law it would be ineffective if it did not bind all who are affected by the conditions prescribed in the code. The power of the President conferred by the statute to fix working conditions would be futile if the conditions as fixed by him were not obligatory on both workers and management. A limitation upon the power of the President, however, which is found in Section 7 (c), must be noted. It reads: "No attempt shall be made to introduce any classification according to the nature of the work involved which might tend to set a maximum as well as a minimum wage." The obligatory force of the code operates only with respect to the conditions in the code. With respect to matters not there included the freedom of action of workers and management is unrestrained.

Having said this much as to the construction of Section 7 (a) and the other labor provisions of the Recovery Act, I shall now pass to a review of what has been done and what has been experienced in the practical application of the law. In passing, I might observe that the Recovery Act with respect to collective bargaining is not entirely new. It is a reaffirmation of the declared policy of the government as set forth in the Norris-LaGuardia Anti-Injunction Law, although the changes in substantive law effected by the latter Act are by no means free from doubt.

A primary tribunal for the adjustment of labor complaints and disputes is within the industry itself. It is the Industrial Relations Committee appointed by the Code Authority in accordance with the order of the Administrator. I have mentioned this body in dealing with the organization of the NRA. It is an agency of the Code Authority designed to handle labor disputes. Under the order of the Administrator it must consist of an equal number of representatives of employers and employees and an impartial chairman. The chairman is appointed by the Administrator upon the failure of the Committee to select one by agreement. If the employees have no truly representative organization then the employee members of the Committee may be nominated by the Labor Advisory Board of the NRA and appointed by the Administrator. The employer representatives are chosen by the Code Authority. The Committee deals with complaints and disputes relating to labor in accordance with rules and regulations issued by the Administrator. Divisional, regional and local adjustment agencies may be established if deemed advisable.

Such an agency within the industry for the adjustment of labor complaints and disputes is in certain major industries of real importance. In other and numerous industries where there has never been any coöperative action of employers in dealing with labor, such a national body is a distinct and unwelcome innovation. In such industries it is considered unnecessary and of no utility whatsoever, and to have a tendency to create labor dissatisfaction and unrest rather than to promote harmonious and satisfactory human relations. Many hundreds of manufacturers throughout the country, operating plants in which labor troubles are unknown, do not desire to subject the relation with their workers to the control of an external authority, even though organized within their own industry. According to their views industrial harmony and peace will be best promoted by leaving to the management of the plant, where it has traditionally belonged, the adjustment of disputes and complaints with the working forces.

The wisdom of constituting such a central body in an industry and placing within its jurisdiction the adjustment of labor complaints and disputes depends on the facts and conditions in such industry. The assumption that all industries and manufacturing plants in the country need an external authority to adjust labor complaints and disputes is obviously without any real foundation. In many industries, the order of the Administrator has the effect of erecting authority without respect to conditions and without reason. Rigid requirements applied to all trades and industries in the interest of uniformity and standardization are not sane regulations. They are, in the worst sense, regimentation.

The labor adjustment committees which the Administrator has established and is establishing must, of course, deal by mediation, conciliation and arbitration. They have no compulsory power. No rules or regulations governing their action have as yet been issued by the Administrator.

Settlement of labor disputes by federal agencies has become of vastly increased importance. Very early in the history of the NRA in dealing with conditions in the major industries, with strikes and threatened strikes, it was found that a special administrative body was essential and for that reason the National Labor Board was created.[4] Decentralized units termed Regional Labor

[4] Executive Order, Dec. 16, 1933, continuing the National Labor Board.—By virtue of the authority vested in me by an Act of Congress, entitled "An Act to encourage national industrial recovery, to foster fair competition, and to provide for the construction of certain useful public works, and for

Boards have been appointed by the National Board. Appeals can be taken from the Regional Boards to the National Labor Board.

While the Board is concerned with disputes that involve violations of Section 7 (a), it also endeavors to settle the more ordinary controversies in which no violation of the statute is involved. On December 16, 1933, a formal Executive Order dealing with the work of the Board was issued. In this order the President stated:

"This objective can only be reached through coöperation on the part of all those associated with industry. In order to develop the greatest degree of coöperation and the highest type of service on the part of management and labor, we urge that all causes of irritation and industrial discontent be removed so far as possible; that all concerned respect the rights of both employers and employees; avoid aggressive action which tends to provoke industrial discord, and strive earnestly and zealously to preserve industrial peace pending

other purposes," approved June 16, 1933 (Public, No. 67, 73rd Cong.), and in order to effectuate the purposes of that Act, it is hereby ordered that:

The National Labor Board, created on August 5, 1933, to "pass promptly on any case of hardship or dispute that may arise from interpretation or application of the President's Reëmployment Agreement," shall continue to adjust all industrial disputes, whether arising out of the interpretation and operation of the President's Reëmployment Agreement or any duly approved industrial code of fair competition, and to compose all conflicts threatening the industrial peace of the country. All action heretofore taken by this Board in the discharge of its functions is hereby approved and ratified.

The powers and functions of this Board shall be as follows:

1 — To settle by mediation, conciliation or arbitration all controversies between employers and employees which tend to impede the purposes of the National Industrial Recovery Act, provided, however, the Board may decline to take cognizance of controversies between employers and employees in any field of trade or industry where a means of settlement, provided for by agreement, industrial code, or Federal law, has not been invoked.

2 — To establish local or regional boards upon which employers and employees shall be equally represented, and to delegate thereto such powers and territorial jurisdiction as the National Labor Board may determine.

3 — To review the determinations of the local or regional boards where the public interest so requires.

4 — To make rules and regulations governing its procedure and the discharge of its functions.

(*Signed*) FRANKLIN D. ROOSEVELT.

the construction and adoption of the Industrial Codes applicable to all business, large and small. Exceptional and peculiar conditions of employment affecting small employers and others whose business circumstances merit special consideration will be handled with due regard to the facts of the situation and with the desire to achieve increased employment and purchasing power."

The function of the Board is to settle labor disputes by mediation, conciliation or arbitration. The submission to the jurisdiction of the Board by labor or management is voluntary. No federal statute regulating trade and industry requires compulsory arbitration. If a controversy is submitted by an employer and employees to the Board for conciliation or mediation, the Board is then vested with authority to consider the case and to make a recommendation as to its solution. Neither the employer nor the employees can be compelled to accept the recommendation of the Board. If, in the consideration of a case, conditions develop which show a violation of law or of a code, the matter may be referred to the Department of Justice for appropriate action.

The National Labor Board and the Regional Boards created by it have no jurisdiction in cases where employers are not operating under a code, either an industrial code or the "blanket code" promulgated by the President.

In the mediation of labor disputes many important decisions have been announced by the National Labor Board. In one of the first cases, that involving the United Textile Workers Union, a regular American Federation of Labor union, and the employer, Berkley Woolen Mills, the Board ruled in its opinion that the refusal of an employer to deal with any organization selected by his employees as their representative constituted a violation of Section 7 (a) of the Recovery Act and of the code for the industry.[5]

Certain principles have been definitely announced by the Board. Some of them are:

The discharge of employees because of their union activity is contrary to Section 7 (a).

The manner of conducting an election (to determine the authorized representatives of employees) is entirely within the discretion of the employees, and the employer in no way can interfere with the conduct of the election.

The initiation of a company union by an employer and the participation by him in its affairs, where such initiation and participation has, in effect, been an interference with the employees' self-organization, or resulted, in fact, in the domination of the organization by the employer, and where the employees have not clearly consented thereto, is unlawful.

It has been pointed out that there is a marginal area of settlement through the influence of the mere existence of the Board. Disputants have settled because it was realized there was a tribunal to which the matter would ultimately have to go.[6]

The supervision of industrial elections held for the purpose of selecting representatives of labor for collective bargaining has become one of the most important functions of the National Labor Board. The advent of federally supervised elections at factories and the secret ballot is so recent that their real significance can-

[5] In the words of the Board: "We rule, therefore, that employees have the right to choose anyone they may wish as their representatives and are not limited in their choice to fellow-employees. We rule, further, that the respondent's refusal to deal with representatives of the employees, unless these representatives are workers in the mill, is an attempt to interfere with and restrain the employees in the designation of their representatives, and is a violation of the code which covers the industry of which respondent is a member, as well as a violation of the Industrial Recovery Act." Decision of the Labor Board, Case No. 28, Sept. 6, 1933.

[6] Release of National Labor Board, No. 3414, Feb. 21, 1934.

not now be measured. They may be of tremendous importance in the union labor movement in America.

Prior to February 1, 1934, the Board did not have the power to compel an election. The manner of the selection of their representatives rested with the employees themselves. The employer, of course, under Section 7 (a) had no right to interfere with such elections or determine the manner in which they should be held.

By Executive Order of February 1, 1934, the President conferred upon the National Labor Board the power of calling and conducting an election upon the request of a substantial number of employees, or any specific group of employees of any plant or business, to select representatives for collective bargaining.

An election is one device for determining the representatives of a majority of the workers for collective bargaining purposes. It is not the exclusive method for making such determination, and need not be employed except in those cases where no other adequate method exists. Where no controversy exists between or among any groups or factions of employees as to which group represents the majority, or where it is conceded by all concerned that a particular group represents the majority of the employees, an election need not be ordered by the Board, despite the fact that a substantial number of employees may request it.

It is only where the petitioning group desires representation through a certain agency, and another group of employees or the employer denies that the agency so designated represents the majority of the employees, that the services of the Board are needed to determine the question in dispute.[7]

An extremely important joint statement of remarkable

[7] Release No. 4118, March 29, 1934.

clarity was issued by Administrator Hugh S. Johnson and Donald R. Richberg, his General Counsel, to put an end to published misconstructions of the Executive Order of the President which empowered the National Labor Board to supervise the conduct of elections. This statement in substance declares that the Executive Order provides a method whereby any specific group of employees or all the employees of a plant or of one employer may select by majority vote representatives clearly empowered to act for the majority in their relations with their employer; that the selection of majority representatives does not restrict or qualify in any way the right of minority groups of employees or of individual employees to deal with their employer. The statement further declares that the purpose of the Executive Order was to provide a definite, workable method for the selection by the majority of any group of employees of their representatives who will thereupon be entitled to recognition as the representatives of the will of the majority of the employees eligible to join in that selection.

This statement further suggested that it had been pointed out frequently that the right of collective bargaining is not the right to obtain a specific contract because a contract must be the result of an agreement and neither employees nor employers can be compelled to enter into a specific contract, but it is to be assumed that if both employer and employee are assured that the representatives of employees have been selected freely and without coercion to represent the desires of a majority of those affected, then any contract resulting from such collective bargaining will stabilize employment conditions and produce the most satisfactory relations possible between employer and employees.

Under Section 7 (a) employers are forbidden to require

as "a condition of employment" that an employee shall either "join a company union" or "refrain from joining, organizing, or assisting a labor organization of his own choosing." The law does not prohibit the existence of a local labor organization, which may be called a company union composed only of the employees of one company, or of a shop committee, to represent the working forces. It does prohibit an employer from requiring as a condition of employment that any employee join a company union and it prohibits the maintenance of a company union, or any other labor organization, by the interference, restraint, or coercion of an employer.

A company union which, as a matter of fact, is the result of coercion by employers has been held illegal in an interpretation of the Railway Labor Act by the Supreme Court.[8] That court, in defining the terms "interference," "influence," and "coercion" as used in the Railway Labor Act, said, "the phrase covers the abuse of relation or opportunity so as to corrupt or override the will" of the workers. The evidence there was so unmistakable that the company had attempted "to corrupt or override the will" of the workers that the court ruled this action to be in definite violation of the Railway Labor Act and hence the company union set up by the railroad was held an illegal organization.

The facts control. The gist of the statute is that it is the exclusive concern of the workers whether or not they shall organize, what form their organization shall take, and the manner in which their representatives shall be designated. There can be no other meaning of the term "self-organization" as used in the Recovery Act. So long as the company union or a shop committee represents the

[8] *Texas and New Orleans Ry.* v. *Brotherhood of Railway Clerks,* 281 U. S. 548 (1930).

uninfluenced choice of a majority of workers in any given plant, the legality of such an organization seems clear.

The vital social importance of the labor provisions of the Act has been accentuated by the recent rapid increase in the number of industrial disputes and strikes throughout the country. Strikes have greatly increased since the passage of the Recovery Act. The *Monthly Labor Review* reports 545 industrial disputes involving 488,393 workers in July, August, and September, 1933, as against 296 disputes involving 104,642 workers in the three months immediately preceding the enactment of the Recovery Act.[9] Conflicts between workers and management were probably never more serious than in the month of May, 1934. Strikes of wide import now exist or are threatened in various parts of the country.

The most critical situation was the threatened automobile strike at Detroit. This struggle strained the provisions of Section 7 (a) to the breaking point. Gigantic forces battled over the issue of open shop versus unionization. The intervention of the President saved the country from the catastrophe of a great strike. The adjustment or truce came by an agreement for the appointment of a mediation board of three members, one a labor representative, one an industry representative, and one neutral, to pass on all questions of representation, discharge, and discrimination. Some of the principles of adjustment are of such general importance that they may well be restated here :

> The employers agree to bargain collectively with the freely chosen representatives of groups and not to discriminate in any way against any employee on the ground of his union labor affiliations.

[9] 37 *Monthly Labor Review,* November, 1933, p. 1139.

If there be more than one group each bargaining committee shall have total membership *pro rata* to the number of men each member represents.

The government makes it clear that it favors no particular union or particular form of employee organization or representation. The government's only duty is to secure absolute and uninfluenced freedom of choice without coercion, restraint or intimidation from any source.

The industry understands that in any reductions or increases of forces, such human relationships as married men with families shall come first, and then seniority, individual skill and efficient service. After these factors have been considered no greater proportion of outside union employees similarly situated shall be laid off than of other employees. By outside union employees is understood a paid-up member in good standing, or anyone legally obligated to pay up. An appeal shall lie in case of dispute on the principles of this paragraph to the Board of Three.

Litigation involving the construction of Section 7 (a) is coming in large volume before the courts. As is usual the courts of original jurisdiction are rendering conflicting opinions. In New York the court doubted that the words of Section 7 (a) confer a right on employees to demand that an employer confer with a union whose members are not exclusively employees of the employer.[10] In Wisconsin the court restrained the manufacturer from "interfering with or imposing any restraint or coercion upon the freedom of its employees in the designation of representatives of their own choice for the purpose of collective bargaining."[11] The construction and application of the Act will remain a matter for controversy and contention until the Supreme Court determines with final authority the meaning and application of the law.

10 *H. B. Rosenthal-Ettlinger Co.* v. *Jos. Schlossberg et al,* N. Y. Supreme Court, Dutchess County, Oct. 12, 1933.

11 *Wisconsin State Fed. of Labor* v. *Simplex Shoe Mfg. Co.* (Cir. Ct. Milwaukee Co., Wis., Oct 13, 1933, No. 131900.)

The *cause celebre* is *United States* v. *Weirton Steel Company* in the United States District Court in Delaware. The government there sought an injunction against the Weirton Steel Company against interference with employees in their free choice of representatives for collective bargaining. It aimed to enjoin the company from requiring employees to participate in a company union and from discharging employees on account of union affiliations and from interfering with employees in their efforts to hold an election to select representatives for collective bargaining. Alleged violations of the Recovery Act and the Iron and Steel Code in resorting to intimidation and coercion of employees were charged in the bill. The validity of Section 7 (a) and the constitutionality of all powers of the NRA were challenged by the steel company. After extended argument the court by an inconclusive opinion has denied a preliminary injunction.[12]

Rational negotiation of the solution of labor differences is too often marred by psychological factors, sometimes subconscious, not always openly expressed, yet real and potent. Not a few officials of organized labor and leaders of industry are swayed by antagonisms and enmities imbedded in human emotions over a long period of years. When clashes come these factors dominate rather than reason or deliberate thought. Instead of negotiating as men engaged in a common enterprise, equally interested in its success, they are warring factions seeking advantage. Labor seeks to conquer and dominate; industry seeks to crush and then dictate. The

[12] May 30, 1934, press notices announce the decision of the U. S. District Court at Wilmington, rejecting the plea for a preliminary injunction on the ground that the Government's pleadings and affidavits disclose that the plaintiff's contentions in fact and in law are seriously disputed. The presiding judge declared that there was not only a "conflict of material facts but a question as to the constitutionality of the NIRA."

Kipling law of the jungle rules these recurring dramas. Until these ugly emotional factors are obliterated from labor conflicts industrial peace is an iridescent dream. What is needed is a new psychology and a new vision. Only changed human hearts and minds will produce durable economic peace. It is a field for a moral and spiritual renovation.

The profit-system and wage-system will endure upon this broad continent for many generations to come. This prophecy seems admissible in view of the essential nature of the national character. Certainly there is now no sign on the horizon of a transition to a substitute system. The two notable national economic establishments of Europe, with their subserviency to enthroned autocracy, are abhorrent to the great mass of Americans. Workers and merchants and manufacturers and professional men and women in this country will not accept a system in which their daily lives and occupations are rigidly regimented by the state unless their present temper and character deeply change. The integrity of the present system will endure and statesmen will evolve new schemes for the government of relations between management and labor. Collective bargaining, which is not new,[13] except as a federal statutory obligation, will remain a master-principle of any scheme of regulation. Its reasonableness and justice and necessity will make it permanent.

Far more significant to the industrial future of America than the legal rights and obligations with respect to collective bargaining, fixed by statute or judicial decisions, will be the spirit and understanding with which collective bargaining is carried on. It will be vain and futile

[13] The legality of collective bargaining has been established for nearly a century. *Commonwealth* v. *Hunt,* 4 Metcalf (Mass.) 111 (1842).

unless both sides to the controversy have a desire to understand and be governed by the existing facts and conditions. Over both sides is the paramount public interest. This public interest demands coöperation and harmonious relations. Management must approach collective bargaining with complete fairness and with a true recognition of the human dignity of labor as well as its economic value. This implies also an insight into the needs of the labor forces and their families for healthful and normal lives. Both parties must deal in the spirit of partnership in a common enterprise. Representatives of labor must act and deal with an insight and understanding of the facts and conditions of the business. They cannot approach the problem on the assumption that management has an unlimited wage-paying capacity on which it can draw at will. Management is in the grip of competitive forces. The products of the plant are in competition for the consumer's dollar with the products of hundreds of other plants, similar and dissimilar, domestic and foreign. The common and paramount interest of management and labor is to keep the plant running to its normal capacity. Harmony and durable peace will depend far less on law than on the psychology of those who participate in the process of collective bargaining.

In the application of Section 7 (a) and the adjustment of labor disputes the NRA and its adjunct the National Labor Board have assumed a herculean task. If their work is to be practicable and effective the functions of mediation, conciliation and arbitration should be confined to industries of national organization and importance. An attempt to deal with all local and isolated cases of labor complaints and troubles will amass a volume of work under which effective functioning will be impossible. In this broad national field, its success even to any substantial degree, will be an immeasurable public service. It is a truth often, but not too often, reiterated that the masses of the people bear the losses which result from industrial conflict. Events of the coming year will determine whether the application of Section 7 (a) will tend to promote that partnership of workers and management considered so essential to economic recovery. If not, the Recovery Act will fail in one of its great objectives, "to induce and maintain united action of labor and management under adequate governmental functions and supervision."

CHAPTER V

THE APPLICATION OF THE ANTI-TRUST PROVISIONS OF THE ACT

THE conditions under which the Recovery Act was prepared were not conducive to careful and precise draftsmanship. Washington in the Spring of 1933 had none of Milton's "quiet air of delightful studies." It was not a place for that calm detachment essential to the penning of great documents in language that is lucid and exact with all their parts related and harmonious. Considering the conditions under which the Recovery Act was drafted and the speed with which it was adopted, it is not a little remarkable that so large a portion of the Act is skillfully and excellently drawn. A grievous exception to this statement, however, is the anti-trust provisions of the Act. They are crudely drawn and create almost insoluble doubt and ambiguity. They are the evident result of political maneuvering and compromise.

Section 5 reads:

> "While this title is in effect (or in the case of a license, while section 4 (a) is in effect) and for sixty days thereafter, any code, agreement, or license approved, prescribed, or issued and in effect under this title, and any action complying with the provisions thereof taken during such period shall be exempt from the provisions of the anti-trust laws of the United States."

That in itself is a plain declaration. Alone it would have a clear and definite operation. By it coöperative action under codes would be distinctly and definitely liberated from the Sherman Act and other anti-trust enactments. Studied and matured plans for coöperative action could be devised by a trade or industry and submitted to the NRA for its consideration. Aided by the counsel of its Law, Labor, Industry, Planning and Consumers Divisions, these submitted plans for concerted action with respect to production and prices could be weighed in the light of the facts and conditions affecting the particular industry and the public. If found promotive of the welfare of the industry as a whole and consistent with the interests of the consuming public, such schemes for coöperative action could be embodied in the approved codes. Such provisions would then be unquestionably legal by virtue of Section 5 of the Act. For clarity and certainty this would be a great advance in dealing with the legality of business transactions.

But Section 3 (a) of the Act radically changes this happy situation. That section makes it unlawful for the President to approve a code if it is designed to promote monopolies or to eliminate or oppress small enterprises or to discriminate against them, or, in the broad terms of the Act, designed to promote monopolistic practices. At the heart of Section 3 (a) was injected the direct proviso: "that such code or codes shall not permit monopolies or monopolistic practices." These provisions are in sharp conflict with Section 5 which suspends the anti-trust laws. Therefore the separate sections of the Act are, on their face, inconsistent and contradictory. They baffle harmonious construction and their application has led to endless controversy and contention.

If the intent and meaning of Section 3 (a) is that any form of coöperative action under codes remains unlawful if it tends to promote monopolies, or to eliminate or oppress small enterprises, or to discriminate against them, or to permit monopolies or monopolistic practices, then the merchants and manufacturers of this country operate under codes in a cloud of the gravest doubt and uncertainty. Those who comply with codes may because of such compliance be subject to injunctional proceedings or even prosecution. The term "monopoly" can be quite readily defined. It embraces business practices which put the supply of a commodity at the mercy of a single private control. But in dealing with the term "monopolistic practices" we are upon an uncharted sea of industrial and commercial activities. The Supreme Court, in interpreting the Sherman law, has held that the term monopolistic practices is synonymous with restraints of trade.[1] Any form of coöperative action in limiting production by agreements for maximum working hours, or for limited plant or production facilities, or for adherence to filed prices, or under covenants against selling below cost, may be held by the courts to be restraints of trade tending to promote monopolies and monopolistic practices and, therefore, not only illegal but criminal. This is not order but chaos.

One escape from the conflict between Sections 5 and 3 (a) would be by a decision that the President has the sole and final discretion to determine in approving a code that the concerted action therein authorized does not promote monopolies or permit monopolistic practices or oppress and discriminate against small enterprises. This theory, which meets with many difficulties, would be criticized as vesting in the President limitless power, but the whole Act was intended to vest in the President limitless and extraordinary powers.[2]

The statute expressly gives the President upon application the power to approve a code or codes of fair competition for the trade or industry "if the President finds . . .

[1] *Standard Oil Company of New Jersey* v. *United States,* 221 U. S., 1 (1910).

[2] See "National Industrial Recovery Act," by Milton Handler, *American Bar Assn. Journal,* Aug. 1933, page 443.

that such code or codes are not designed to promote monopolies or to eliminate or oppress small enterprises and will not operate to discriminate against them, and will tend to effecuate the policy of this title: *Provided,* That such code or codes shall not permit monopolies or monopolistic practices." The President is thus charged with the responsibility of examining a code in the light of the facts and conditions of the industry, and determining whether or not it will promote or foster monopolies or monopolistic practices. These are inquiries involving questions of fact as well as of law. If the President finds that the code does not violate this section, and upon that finding, makes the decision to approve the code, his action is final. The code immediately takes effect. From that moment the remedy is an application for the modification of the code. While the code is in force and effect it would seem that all provisions of the anti-trust laws applying to action under the approved code, while unrepealed, should in reason be considered suspended. That appears a reasonable interpretation of the whole Act.

It should be noted that so far as the Recovery Act is concerned, the exemption from the anti-trust laws with respect to concerted action is only effective as to provisions in a code approved by the President. We are dealing with codes of fair competition. It is clear that only such practices as promote fair competition should be embodied in codes. Is the President the final judge of those practices in any trade or industry that will promote fair competition? Consider for instance the matter of price-fixing. The President may find from a study of the facts and conditions in any trade or industry that disastrous price-cutting, one of the destructive practices condemned by the Recovery Act, is demoralizing the industry. He may find that such demoralization is injurious to the public interest. He may find that the disastrous price-cutting is leading to practices detrimental to consumers. He may find that the price-fixing practices will tend to stabilize prices and that this will be in the interest of both producers and consumers and will tend to promote the public welfare. His decision in effect will be that in his judgment the practice of price-fixing by the particular trade or industry about to be placed under the code is not a monopolistic practice. Will the courts upset this decision and invalidate the code? If the provisions in codes with respect to price-fixing are to be held illegal by the courts, then the logical result must be that the courts will condemn all of the other practices authorized by codes which hitherto have been considered offenses under the anti-trust laws.

Under Section 3 (a) authorizing the President to approve codes, he acts only upon the application of the industry. He can, however, under Section 3 (d), as enacted by Congress, upon his own initiative prescribe and approve a code of fair competition for the trade or industry.

In venturing this provisional and tentative interpretation of the whole Act, so far as it deals with offenses hitherto illegal under the anti-trust laws, as one that vests with finality in the President the power to determine what are proper provisions in a code, it should be clearly noted that we are dealing with construction, not constitutionality. We are discussing the meaning of the measure as enacted, not the power of the Congress to enact it. Nor are we here discussing the wisdom or policy of vesting so vast a power in the President. We are concerned only with answering the question: What is the true interpretation and application of the anti-trust provisions of the Recovery Act? If the sound construction of the whole Act is that the President has the power finally to determine the reasonableness and validity of the provisions of a code with respect to monopolies and monopolistic practices and their effect on small enterprises, then the power of the Congress to vest such vast authority in the President is another grave problem which must meet the acid test of judicial review.

A study of the whole Act fortifies the conclusion that a wide measure of concerted action by industry was deemed an essential part of the whole legislative scheme. The primary purpose of the Act was to enable the organization of industry among trade groups under adequate governmental supervision and sanction. The anti-trust laws were a restriction upon such coöperative efforts and without an exemption from their provisions the Act would be "absolutely a mere gesture and ineffective."[3]

In his Message to the Congress on May 17, 1933, the President stated:

"One of the great restrictions upon such coöperative efforts up to this time has been our anti-trust laws. They were properly designed as the means to cure the great evils of monopolistic price-fixing. They could certainly be retained as a permanent assurance that the old evils of unfair competition shall never return. But the public interest will be served if, with the authority and under the guidance of Government, private industries are permitted to make agreements and codes insuring fair competition. However, it is necessary, if we thus limit the operation of anti-trust laws to their original purpose, to provide a rigorous licensing power in order to meet rare cases of non-coöperation and abuse. Such a safeguard is indispensable."

[3] Statement by Senator Wagner at Hearing before House Committee on Ways and Means, May 18-20, 1933, page 93.

In a later statement the President declared:

"We are relaxing some of the safeguards of the anti-trust laws. The public must be protected against the abuses that led to their enactment, and to this end, we are putting in place of old principles of unchecked competition some new government controls. They must above all be impartial and just. Their purpose is to free business—not to shackle it—and no man who stands on the constructive forward-looking side of his industry has anything to fear from them. To such men the opportunities for individual initiative will open more amply than ever. Let me make it clear, however, that the anti-trust laws still stand firmly against monopolies that restrain trade and price-fixing which allows inordinate profits or unfairly high prices." [4]

Senator Wagner, who led the debate for the Recovery Act in the Senate, declared that "the first title of the bill deals with the problem of order in trade and industry and involves primarily a reconsideration of the traditional attitude toward competition as embodied in the anti-trust laws." [5] Similarly, in the House, in opposing an amendment introduced by Senator Borah to prohibit price-fixing, it was stated that the law "was offered to stabilize industry, to increase employment, to limit production, to maintain maximum hours of employment and minimum wage scales. All will fail if agreements cannot be made as to prices." [6]

The provisions of the Act itself plainly indicate the unquestioned purpose of Congress to enable manufacturers to enter upon a wide field of concerted action.

The statute must be interpreted as a whole and its various provisions all given a meaning and effect.

Section 1 declares that one of the cardinal purposes of

[4] Excerpt from Bulletin No. 1, June 16, 1933.
[5] Congressional Record, June 7, 1933, page 5254.
[6] Congressional Record, June 10, 1933, page 5736.

the Act was "to provide for the general welfare by promoting the organization of industry for the purpose of coöperative action among trade groups." The same section affirms the purpose "to eliminate unfair competitive practices."

In Section 3 it is said that a code "shall be the standard of fair competition for such trade or industry," and again Section 3, paragraph (*a*), refers to conditions attached to a code "for the protection of . . . competitors." Again in paragraph (*b*) of Section 4 reference is made to destructive price-cutting as an activity contrary to the policy of the title.

Two of the prime objects of the NRA are to eliminate cut-throat underselling and to end unfair competitive practices. As stated by Senator Wagner in a Senate hearing, "the main purpose of this legislation is to rationalize competition." There can be no question that one of the purposes of the law is to make competition open and fair and consonant with the interest of manufacturers as well as consumers and to legalize methods that will make this possible.

The statute legalizes agreements and coöperative action of manufacturers in curtailing and controlling production because it legalizes agreements under codes to fix maximum working hours, minimum wages, and other working conditions. It seems clear that unless the provisions of the Sherman law and other anti-trust enactments have no operation with respect to the provisions of codes, then the Recovery Act is emasculated and made futile. Unless agreements of an industry embodied in codes with respect to prices and production were to be permitted under the new régime then there was no point in suspending the anti-trust laws. The intent of Congress to suspend the anti-trust laws with respect to codes as clearly and positively declared in Section 5 cannot be read out of the Act.

The Supreme Court, in its decisions under the Sherman law, has ruled that the phrase "monopolistic practices," which is the language of the Recovery Act, is a synonym for restraints of trade.[7] If it is now to be held that the Recovery Act forbids monopolistic practices and, therefore, forbids any restraint of trade, then the whole Act is practically vitiated. There is no doubt whatever that approved codes contain many agreements which under old legal principles should be condemned as restraints of trade. If the statute is given a narrow construction, then its efficacy in permitting association and coöperative action of merchants and manufacturers is ended.

Of what avail is it to give the President the power to "establish an industrial planning and research agency to aid in carrying out his functions under this title" [Section 2 (*b*)], unless a wide measure of concerted action in industry is contemplated by the Act and exempted from the Sherman law? The outstanding vice of the Sherman law is the uncertainty of what it forbids and what it permits.

Disregarding any conflict in the Act with respect to concerted and coöperative action of merchants and manufacturers, the President has approved a vast number of codes which modify or abridge the freedom of the individual in the industry to control his own production and to make his own prices and terms of sale. Code provisions which have been framed and are widely in effect have to do with such matters as (1) the fixing of minimum prices; (2) prohibitions against selling below individual cost of production or below a reasonable cost;

[7] *Standard Oil Company of New Jersey* v. *United States,* 221 U. S., 1 (1911).

(3) open price arrangements; and (4) limitation on production and on measure of productive capacity. Mechanisms for price-fixing are present in a vast number of codes.

Under codes business groups have outlawed individual competitive practices peculiarly disastrous to their profitable operations. In some instances members of an industry by concerted action are privileged to fix prices outright; in others they may impose minimum prices upon all members of the trade; they are permitted under the codes to restrict output and to limit the introduction of new productive machinery. In many codes now in existence the initial decision as to what the minimum price shall be is determined by the Code Authority. The Administrator of the NRA reserves the power to veto or suspend any price to which he takes exception. The technique for fixing prices differs in the various codes. The codes disclose an astounding array of devices for the initiation and stabilization of prices. "Fair and reasonable prices" are referred to in many codes. Uniform cost accounting systems are established by the Code Authority which can be used in determining the proper level of minimum prices. Prohibitions against selling an article below its cost of production constitute the most common price-control device and it is found in over one hundred codes. Since each producer is forbidden to sell below his own individual cost of production, that cost constitutes his own minimum price. In recent codes the provisions against selling below cost of production have been modified so that the cost factor is not the individual cost of the producer, but a reasonable cost for the whole industry established by the Code Authority. Other recent codes contain provisions for price-fixing which operate only in an emergency.

Open-price provisions exist in a vast number of codes. Codes with open-price plans typically require that within a specified period after the effective date the members of the industry must file with the Code Authority or some other designated body and publish to the trade the prices, discounts, and terms of sale on which they are transacting business. Thereafter, until revisions of these schedules have been duly put into effect, except in some cases with express permission, the members are forbidden to carry on business, at prices or on terms other than those filed. NRA codes have prescribed open-pricing for scores of industries that have never employed it before. Various methods appear in code provisions for concerted action to restrict production or productive capacity. Under some of these methods production control depends upon the allotment of production quotas to individual members of the industry. The fixed limits on the number of hours per week during which machines can be operated is a direct limitation on production. Provisions for the limitation of new capacity appear in a considerable number of approved codes and in a variety of forms. The arrangement can be described generally by saying that no member of an industry may expand his present productive capacity, either by replacement of existing facilities or by the construction of new plant, without first obtaining the consent of the Administrator.

There is no question that existing codes approved by the President have given the force of law to numerous activities which prior to the passage of the Recovery Act were considered as criminal under the anti-trust laws.

If the validity of codes with respect to coöperative action and its effect on small enterprises and the public welfare is subject to judicial review, then we may hope that the attitude of the courts towards this new order of restricted competition under codes will prove to be modern and liberal.

It is a matter of common knowledge that in recent decisions there has been a decided relaxation of the severity of the Sherman law. In dealing with price control or production control devices under codes, it seems clear that the courts should not decree their condemnation unless from a painstaking and exhaustive study of the facts it appears that the public is injuriously affected. Only in plain and flagrant cases, where it unquestionably appears that the conditions tend to establish a monopoly, or directly and actually oppress or discriminate against small enterprises, should the provisions of the codes be held unlawful.

Recent Supreme Court decisions have established that intelligently regulated competition and public interest are not always in conflict. In a recent case the Court held that trade association activities directed to the collection and dissemination of trade statistics were not in violation of the Sherman law.[8] In another recent case, the Court recognizes the practical necessity of intelligent coöperative action by competitors.[9]

Under certain decisions of the federal courts concerted action for the prevention of disastrous price-cutting in itself has been determined not to be violative of the anti-trust laws. The modern doctrine is well stated in one of these decisions:

"Restriction of competition may not include a fair and reasonable attempt to avoid loss by trade agreements which are aimed to prevent nothing but the cutting of rates below the reasonable expense of production and reasonable profit thereon. . . A mere attempt to obtain a fair profit, even

[8] *Maple Flooring Mfg. Assn.* v. *United States,* 268 U. S. 536 (1924).
[9] *Appalachian Coals* v. *United States,* 288 U. S. 334 (1932).

by an agreement not to undersell, must be tested by the measure of what would be a fair price under competition, and it must be determined whether the centralization or control of the output is intended or does accomplish any interference with the free action of independent parties who might compete, or with the security to the public of all the benefits to which they are entitled, over and above the reasonable cost of production and reasonable profit." [10]

A distinction exists in the cases between coöperative efforts to stabilize prices on the one hand and efforts to curtail production and unduly increase prices on the other. The mere fact that activities or provisions which are lawful might be turned to unlawful ends is not enough in itself to bring about their condemnation. Even prior to NRA the courts were no longer indiscriminately forcing the drastic competitive system upon each and every business. Rather the application of the anti-trust laws was deemed to require the careful consideration of the conditions of the particular business before the court. Coöperation and concerted action which might have constituted a violation of the law in one industry under certain circumstances might be proper and legal in another industry in the light of its different circumstances. A widespread recognition prevailed that intelligent coöperation among competitors was not necessarily in conflict with public welfare and under some circumstances might promote the general good.

Organized labor is vitally interested in the problems involved in the application of the anti-trust laws under codes. Union activities designed to promote the interest of labor have been subject to frequent attacks under the anti-trust laws. Strikes which have been deemed declared for wrongful purposes, attended with boycotts and

[10] *Fonotipia, Ltd.* v. *Bradley*, 171 Fed. 958 (1909).

interferences with production or interference with contract relations and other activities which directly affected interstate commerce, have been declared unlawful and enjoined. If the anti-trust laws are now relaxed with respect to concerted action of merchants and manufacturers, are they also relaxed with relation to the activities of trade unions? Such activities would be limited, of course, to action taken in the performance of provisions in an approved code.

We are dealing with provisions in codes and with the operation of the anti-trust laws with respect to codes. There is a wide field for the operation of the anti-trust laws which has not been limited by this statute. The operation of the statute against the creation of monopolies by mergers and consolidations is not changed. The prohibition in the Clayton Act against holding companies and inter-corporate stock holdings is unaffected by the Recovery Act. The provisions of the Clayton Act regarding price discrimination and exclusive dealing arrangements and tying agreements remain unchanged. The jurisdiction of the Federal Trade Commission is reaffirmed by the new law. The statute specifically provides that "nothing in this title shall be construed to impair the powers of the Federal Trade Commission under such Act, as amended."

In dealing with the reasonableness and justness and necessity of the various provisions in codes with respect to concerted action, we must deal with the facts and conditions of the trade or industry to which they apply. What is meat for one industry is poison for another. Evils of unrestrained competition virulent and destructive in one industry may be non-existent in another. A price-control system for the steel industry would be wholly inapplicable to the automobile industry. A production-limitation plan might fit the coal industry but be absurd if applied to the manufacture of shoes, garments, jewelry, or a thousand other articles. There are many trades and industries in which nationally organized concerted or coöperative action is not suited to the existing facts and conditions. The regulations may be just and reasonable in one code and unreasonable and wholly unnecessary in another. Circumstances and conditions are here the basis of a sound judgment.

The curtailment or amelioration of cut-throat competition was no doubt one of the prime purposes of the Recovery Act. It was intended that rules for the restraint of such competition were in the first instance to be initiated by the trade or industry and then submitted to the NRA for its approval. All such rules and provisions must, of course, be subjected to the test of the public welfare. The evident intention of the Act was to have the NRA and the President represent the public in determining whether the schemes for concerted action were consistent with the general welfare.

The new coöperative methods are not the destruction of competition or individualism but their conservation. Competition in energy, ingenuity, initiation, resourcefulness will continue—competition in the aggressiveness, daring and strategy of management; competition in new products, new styles, models and new methods of production, in quality of product and salesmanship and service. Rational restraints on cut-throat competition are not undue restraints on individualism. "Individualism is what makes coöperation worth while."

The sensational Darrow report declaring that codes are oppressing small merchants is now before the country. The fires of controversy are extremely hot. Mental energies are being consumed in emotion rather than used in deliberate thought and discrimination. As a result of the Darrow report there will no doubt be and there should be a critical and rigid reëxamination of existing codes and a penetrating scrutiny as to their effect on smaller enterprises and on the consuming public. Such a study must be based on the facts and conditions in each industry in which the code is operating. Real evils must be extirpated, small merchants protected and actual injustices to consumers prevented, so far as possible, but in planning and working to that end the good under codes must not be destroyed. To condemn all codes containing provisions for the stabilization of prices or for restrictions on production because of the unsparing assault on the NRA found in the Darrow report would be altogether irrational and unsound.

If the Recovery Act does not in an important way enlarge the freedom of association and coöperation of merchants and manufacturers, if it does not mark an end to the era of disorganized industry and cut-throat competition in many major industries, the experiment has all been in vain. It is a futile gesture if it is to have no real restraining effect on the legally compelled economic warfare which preceded the passage of the Act.

The Supreme Court may hold the entire Act unconstitutional. It may on the contrary uphold its validity as to transactions in and affecting interstate and foreign commerce. In that event the duty of construing and applying the anti-trust clauses of the Act will fall upon that Court. If the Court holds that the dominant provisions are found in Section 3 (a) forbidding monopolies and monopolistic practices and oppression of small enterprises; if it reaches the conclusion that price-controlling and production-limitation devices in approved codes are, after approval by the President, subject to judicial review as to their legality, and are illegal if they constitute restraints of trade such as hitherto have been condemned by many courts under the anti-trust laws; then the NRA should close its office. Thenceforward it would be only a referee in the old game of dog eat dog.

CHAPTER VI

THE ADMINISTRATION AND ENFORCEMENT OF CODES

WE ARE now treading upon firmer ground. The provisions of the Recovery Act as to the administration and enforcement of codes have at least the merits of certainty and consistency. We are also entering a field where discussion is less controversial. All will agree that codes should be strictly administered and enforced. A code not uniformly applied is vicious and harmful. It penalizes the honest merchant or manufacturer who complies with the code, and rewards with a competitive advantage the dissenter or chiseler who fails to comply with its provisions; "those who," to use the words of President Roosevelt, "by declining to follow the rules of the game, seek to gain an unfair advantage over those who live up to the rules." Dissenters and violators render a code futile and demoralize industry.[1]

Violations of codes are both open and direct and indirect and under cover. No doubt some violations are not deliberate but occur from a misconstruction of the code where the language is doubtful or ambiguous. The problem of preventing violations and maintaining a uniform compliance with all codes in the face of human ingenuity and selfishness is now the almost superhuman task of the NRA.

An elaborate machinery exists for enforcing compliance. The primary procedure is within the industry itself, functioning through the Code Authority. Under important codes the code has regional and subordinate divisions and agencies. The administration of codes is

[1] See *On Our Way,* by Franklin D. Roosevelt (1933), page 77. John Day Co.

a part of industrial self-government. These industrial adjustment agencies seek first to establish the fact of violation of a code and then to persuade the violator to mend his ways and adjust the complaint. They deal through conferences and by persuasion. Ultimately responsible, however, under the administrative system, is the NRA. The NRA maintains a supervision and control over administration and enforcement with the avowed purpose to see that all codes are uniformly and fairly applied. When industrial procedure fails the coercive power of the government is invoked.

When a complaint is filed with the Code Authority that a member of the industry is indulging in practices in violation of a code, the first step is a careful investigation of the facts. The company that is the subject of the complaint is summoned to appear before the Code Authority, or one of its regional or subordinate agencies, with which the complaint is filed. Efforts are made to secure adjustment by discussion and agreement. Every opportunity is given for voluntary compliance. If these efforts fail a citation is issued to the firm to appear at a formal hearing before the Code Authority. If the matter is heard by a regional or subordinate agency and adjustment fails, then the case is submitted to the central Code Authority. The Code Authority will review the record, determine the guilt or innocence, and in the event of guilt prescribe the procedure and penalties. The Code Authority has no compulsory power. If all of this procedure fails, the case must go to the governmental agency for compulsory action.

Compliance and enforcement through governmental adjustment agencies is completely organized. State Directors are primarily concerned with the enforcement of codes. These State Directors have their staff of field workers for the investigation of complaints. In the first instance the action of these governmental agencies is not of a coercive or compulsory nature. They seek to secure adjustments by the instruction and education of those subject to the code as to their responsibilities. They invoke the pressure of opinion within the industry. Their procedure is one of conciliation, mediation and arbitration. Where all other means have failed, they report the cases of non-compliance to the NRA in Washington.

All this governmental regional organization is a part of the Compliance Division of the NRA under direction of the National Compliance Director. Its function, according to official announcements, is to fill the gap in industrial self-government. To the extent required, it will act for an industry while the industry is organizing to handle compliance problems for itself; or where an industry in a certain territory has no Industrial Adjustment Agencies; or where an industry, though organized to handle trade practice complaints, has no machinery to handle labor complaints; or where the industry fails to carry through in its efforts to adjust a complaint; or where for any other reason it is necessary for the governmental rather than the industrial system to act. When an industry is completely organized to adjust all complaints, it may still be advantageous, according to the NRA regulations, for it to call upon NRA to supplement its functioning. Thus, the preliminary investigation of some complaints may be made at the request of an Industrial Adjustment Agency by a regional governmental agency and the facts reported to the Industrial Agency. It is often reiterated that in dealing with compliance and enforcement the fundamental theory underlying the

NRA is industrial self-discipline with government partnership.[2]

Ultimately, all unadjusted complaints reported up through an industry by Industrial Adjustment Agencies will be referred to the Compliance Division of the NRA in Washington, as will all unadjusted complaints reported up by the State Directors. If the National Compliance Director is unable to effect an adjustment, such complaints will be referred to the National Compliance Board. If it is unable to effect compliance it will turn the case over to the appropriate enforcement agency of the Federal Government—either the Department of Justice or the Federal Trade Commission. These departments will invoke the sanctions provided by law or take all action within their power to enforce compliance with the statute and the codes.[3]

Disputes under codes are classified as trade practice complaints and labor disputes. Most industries operating under codes are at present organized to handle trade practice complaints. Labor disputes present much more difficult problems and few industries are today nationally organized to handle such complaints. Supplementing the NRA is the National Labor Board with its specialized function for the settlement of labor disputes.

Where the prevention of violations fails through the methods of mediation and persuasion, and through the pressure of the Code Authority and the NRA, then the basis and necessity for judicial action arise. Enforcement by judicial proceedings may take several forms. The most important is the injunctive remedy by and in the name of the United States to restrain violations.

[2] NRA Bulletin No. 7. Manual for Adjustment of Complaints by State Directors and Code Authorities.

[3] NRA Bulletin No. 7.

The Recovery Act vests district courts of the United States with jurisdiction to prevent and restrain violations of any code of fair competition and imposes the duty upon district attorneys, in their respective districts, under the direction of the Attorney General, to institute proceedings in equity to prevent and restrain violations. This procedure has already been invoked in a large number of cases. The jurisdiction of the federal courts to enjoin violations of codes is not exclusive. In a case in Wisconsin it was held that the state courts have jurisdiction to enforce the President's Reëmployment Agreement, and in doing so they do not invade the jurisdiction of the federal courts.[4]

An interesting case,[5] testing the validity of production limitations in a code, arose in the lumber industry in the Northwest. The Willamette Valley Lumber Company, the owner of a sawmill, filed a bill in equity to enjoin the Code Authority of the West Coast Lumber Code from enforcing an order allocating a certain number of board feet to each of the mills operating in the district. The complaining company refused to accept its quota under the allotment of production and openly declared its intention to operate its mill free from such restriction. The court denied an injunction against the enforcement of the order of the Code Authority, but took under advisement the question of the validity of the penalties provided in the Recovery Act. The decision refusing to restrain the enforcement of the order of the Code Authority was based upon the grave situation of the lumber industry. In 1928 the mills in this district were operated on the basis of 72 per cent normal, but production had

[4] *Wisconsin State Federation of Labor* v. *Simplex Shoe Mfg. Co.*, Wisconsin Circuit Court, Milwaukee County, Oct. 13, 1933.

[5] *Willamette Valley Lumber Co.* v. *Watzek*, U. S. Dist. Ct. of Oregon, 5 Fed. Supp., 689 (1934).

dropped to 19.8 per cent by the end of 1932; and in 1929 over 95,000 persons were employed, while at the close of 1933, only 30,000 persons were working.

The court, holding that the emergency order was constitutional, made this statement:

"Unfortunately, distribution of allotment requires some mills to make greater sacrifices in productive capacity than others, but this appears to be unavoidable by reason of the diversity in mill operation. However, it is obvious that the administrative agencies have adopted a plan of distribution which, while not perfect, is the most likely to prevent complete disaster to the lumber industry, a plan by which all mills are in one classification, and which does not, in the judgment of the court, arbitrarily discriminate against any mill unit."

In New York an attempt was made to enforce the minimum price provisions of a code and it failed.[6] The plaintiffs were "call, deliver and credit" cleaners; the defendants were "cash and carry" cleaners. After investigation as to the cost of service the officials of the NRA were not willing to allow any extra rate charge for the extra service. The court overruled this finding, saying:

"If this law means that NIRA has the power to compel a man whose service is worth 40 cents, to charge 75 cents for it, so that his customers will leave him and deal with his competitor, whose service is worth 75 cents, then it is unconstitutional."

The court further states, however, that this was undoubtedly not the meaning of the law, and upon that ground refused an injunction to enforce the minimum price rules.

Directly contrary to the ruling of the New York state

[6] *Cleaners and Dyers Board of Trade, Inc.* v. *Spotless Dollar Cleaners, Inc.*, Supreme Court of N. Y. (Feb. 19, 1934.)

court is the decision of the United States District Court of the Southern District of New York in a case involving the same controversy.[7] The federal court discussed at length the facts with regard to cost and concluded that the Code Authority made a correct finding in determining that the cost of one service was substantially the equivalent of the other. Interstate commerce was involved in the case, the court held, because garments picked up in New York were processed in New Jersey. Governmental price-fixing in such transactions was sustained as a means reasonably adopted by Congress in an emergency to overcome destructive price-cutting declared to be a burden upon interstate commerce in the dry cleaning industry.

In one case the court enjoined wage cuts because they lowered the wages below the minimum provided in the motion picture code.[8] A similar injunction was denied in another case on the ground that the wages and hours were not subject to federal regulation.[9] In still another case it was held that not all oil producers are engaged in interstate commerce or in transactions affecting interstate commerce and, therefore, all are not subject to regulation by the Federal Government.[10] Another very recent decision is that the prohibition of the use of premiums in the sale of petroleum products under the petroleum code is invalid as to a retailer operating exclusively within a single state.[11] About the same time another court

[7] *United States* v. *Spotless Dollar Cleaners Inc.,* U. S. Dist. Ct., So. Dist. of N. Y., Eq. No. 77-207, Mar. 31, 1934, 104 CCH 7130.

[8] *Brodsky,* et al, v. *Sharbu Operating Co. Inc.,* Supreme Court, New York County, N. Y. Feb. 7, 1934.

[9] *United States* v. *Bob Lieto,* U. S. Dist. Ct. No. Dist. of Texas, Feb. 16, 1934.

[10] *Amazon Petroleum Corp.* v. *Railroad Comm. of Texas,* U. S. Dist. Ct., East. Dist. of Texas, 5 Fed. Supp. 639 (1934).

[11] *United States* v. *Suburban Motor Serv. Corp.,* U. S. Dist. Ct., No. Dist. of Ill., East. Div., 5 Fed. Supp. 798 (1934).

held that the giving of premiums with the sale of gasoline constituted an unfair method of competition under the Petroleum Code.[12] It was decided in this latter case that the rules forbidding premiums were not in violation of the Due Process clause of the Constitution and that premiums could be prohibited in intra-state commerce because of the effect of the practice on inter-state commerce.

Suits for injunction in the lower courts by the government are multiplying and further conflicting decisions will be handed down until the Supreme Court finally adjudges the validity and interpretation of the Recovery Act. The existing judicial interpretation of the statute is a maze of conflict and uncertainty. A distinguished judge plagued by a similar judicial conflict ruefully remarked:

> ". . . It is quite impossible to establish any rule from the decided cases; we must step from tuft to tuft across the morass." [13]

A question of prime importance has arisen as to the right of a private dealer or manufacturer to maintain a suit to restrain a violation of a code. It has been held in a number of cases that a private citizen has no standing in court to ask for an injunction because the National Recovery Act [Section 3 (c)] contemplates that actions to restrain violations of codes of fair competition shall be brought by and in the name of the United States acting through its district attorneys.[14] This, of course, refers

[12] *Victor* v. *Ickes*, Supreme Court of the District of Columbia, December 1, 1933.

[13] Judge Learned Hand in *Hutchinson* v. *Chase & Gilbert*, 45 Fed. (2d), 142.

[14] *Chicago Flexible Shaft Co.* v. *Katz Drug Co.*, U. S. Dist. Ct. of Delaware, Feb. 23, 1934; *Purvis* v. *Bazemore*, 5 Fed. Supp. 230 (1934); *John Stanley* v. *Peabody Coal Co.*, U. S. Dist. Ct., So. Dist. of Ill., Eq. No. 1239, 5 Fed. Supp. 612 (1934).

to proceedings for injunction to restrain violations of a code. Private injunctive relief is undoubtedly the proper remedy for a member of an industry who claims that a code is illegal and that its operation is irreparably injuring his business.

The question of private injunctive relief to restrain the violation of a code is not free from doubt. It can well be argued, upon many analogies in connection with other federal statutes, that the omission from the Recovery Act of provisions for private injunctional relief does not of itself preclude such a remedy. Since the Act is designed to protect members of the industry from unfair practices by other members, this injunctive relief would seem appropriate to prevent code violations that directly and in a special manner injure the business of a particular member of the industry. Codes exist for the benefit of the industry as well as for the protection of the general public. Government officials cannot be relied upon promptly to protect the members of every trade and industry in the country that are especially injured by the violation of a code. If codes are to be effectively enforced the private right to injunctional relief seems expedient if not essential.

Instances of private relief of this character under other federal statutes are quite numerous. A private complainant would not, of course, be entitled to equitable relief if he suffers merely in common with other members of the public.[15] Injunctions have been granted to private parties under the federal anti-trust laws where special injury was shown.[16] Under the Railway Labor Act, injunctional relief was accorded railway employees

[15] *Massachusetts* v. *Mellon,* 262 U. S. 447, 488 (1933); *Calkins* v. *Westervelt,* 214 Fed. 415 (W. D. Mich. 1913).

[16] *Mannington* v. *Hocking Valley Ry. Co.,* 183 Fed. 133 (C.C.S.D. Ohio, 1910), and cases cited.

restraining their employers from interfering with employee representatives, although no express provision for this remedy had been made.[17] The Interstate Commerce Act includes elaborate provisions for its enforcement, yet its failure to provide for private injunctive rights to restrain discrimination and to require adequate service has not prevented the granting of such relief.[18]

By recent announcement the NRA officially decrees that a particular dealer or manufacturer especially injured by the violation of a code has no remedy except by application either for exemption from the code or its modification. An instance of this exemptive action is that taken with respect to employers of less than five persons and employers located in towns of less than 2,500 people. They were exempted from the blanket code.[19] Similar action, it has been announced, is in contemplation with respect to the exemption of service trades from complete regimentation.[20]

We have now considered procedure for injunction as an instrument for the enforcement of codes. There is another phase of judicial enforcement. This involves the application of the penalty clauses of the Recovery Act. In substance these are:

Violation of any provision of a code in any transaction affecting interstate or foreign commerce is a misdemeanor, punishable by a fine of not more than $500 for each offense.

[17] *Texas and New Orleans Railway Co.* v. *Railway Clerks,* 281 U. S. 548 (1930).

[18] *In re* Lennon, 166 U. S. 548, 553, 554 (1897); *Toledo Ry. Co.* v. *Pennsylvania Co.,* 54 Fed. 730, 732 (C.C.N.D. Ohio, 1893) *Louisville & Nashville Ry. Co.* v. *Cook Brewing Co.,* 223 U. S. 70 (1912); *Interstate Stock Yards Co.* v. *Indianapolis Union Ry. Co.,* 99 Fed. 472 (C.C.D. Indiana, 1900); *Stephens* v. *Ohio State Telephone Co.,* 240 Fed. 759 (N.D. Ohio, 1917); *Kroger Gro. & Baking Co.* v. *Retail Clerks,* 250 Fed. 890 (E.D. Mo. 1918); *Federal Trade Commission* v. *Beech Nut Co.,* 257 U. S. 441, 453 (1922); *Moore* v. *New York Cotton Exchange,* 270 U. S. 593 (1926).

[19] NRA Release No. 1341.

[20] *Chicago Tribune,* May 29, 1934.

Each day the violation continues is deemed a separate offense.

Violation of any rule or regulation prescribed by the President is punishable by a fine of not to exceed $500, or imprisonment for not to exceed six months, or both.

Any violation of a code that affects interstate commerce is deemed an unfair method of competition within the meaning of the Federal Trade Commission Act, as amended.

It has been suggested as a singular fact that the National Industrial Recovery Act provides no penalty for the violation of the Act itself. The only offenses denounced in the Act are those for the violation of a code approved by the President, and for disobedience to the rules and regulations prescribed by the President for carrying out the purposes of the Act.

Prosecutions have been instituted under the provisions of the Act which in effect make every code of fair competition a criminal statute. The first case to reach a decision was *United States* v. *Hercules Gas Stations.*[21] Fines were imposed upon a plea of guilty by defendants in a criminal prosecution for violation of the Petroleum Code by a retailer who had not signed the code. Regarding this case Secretary Ickes said: "The case was the first criminal prosecution under the Oil Code to reach a final conclusion and represents a signal victory. The outcome of the case is most gratifying. It should serve as a warning to other violators of any provisions of the Code."

Criminal actions for enforcement of the penalties of the statute have not been as numerous as proceedings to enjoin violations of codes. An injunction is the important remedy under judicial enforcement. There is no doubt that enforcement of codes through court action has been impeded by the grave doubts that have arisen

21 United States District Court, Eastern District of New York, Dec. 1, 1933.

as to the interpretation and constitutionality of many provisions of the Recovery Act.

The enforcement policy of the NRA in encouraging and promoting self-enforcement by industry through its own adjustment agencies is unquestionably based on wisdom and expediency. The NRA encourages conferences and persuasion and every opportunity for voluntary compliance. The work of industrial adjustment agencies is supplemented where government intervention is necessary. Administration is decentralized and the government agencies are so located that cases of violations can be investigated and dealt with in or near the communities in which they arise. Only in flagrant cases of violations of codes, or their avowed defiance, is the power of the courts invoked.

Indirect methods of the NRA to enforce compliance are generally known and are of great importance. One drastic indirect method is the exclusion from government bidding of dissenters from codes.

On March 14, 1934, an Executive Order was issued providing that "all invitations to bidders hereafter promulgated by or in behalf of any Executive Department or independent establishment or other agency or instrumentality of the United States, including government-owned and government-controlled corporations, shall contain a provision to the effect that no bid will be considered unless it includes or is accompanied by a certificate duly executed by the bidder, stating that the bidder is complying with and will continue to comply with each approved code of fair competition to which he is subject, and if engaged in any trade or industry for which there is no approved code of fair competition, then stating that as to such trade or industry he has become a party to and is complying with and will continue to comply with an agreement with the President under Section 4 (a) of the National Industrial Recovery Act."

The Order provides that no bid which does not comply with the foregoing requirements shall be considered or accepted. All contracts and purchase orders are to contain similar provisions as are contracts and purchase orders authorized by any state, municipal corporation, local subdivision or corporation in connection with projects carried out or to be carried out wholly or in part with funds loaned or granted by any agency of the United States. A provision for a penalty of $500 fine or imprisonment not to exceed six months, or both, is made for any person falsely certifying as to compliance in any proposal, contract or order. Bidders for government contracts are required to certify that they purchase their materials and supplies only from concerns operating under codes. These, in turn, must certify as to the source of their materials. This ingenious enforcement device is an endless chain. It is a striking illustration of the latent extrajudicial powers of government to coerce compliance with its regulations of industry.

The validity of this method of enforcing codes has been seriously questioned, although the Attorney General has definitely expressed the opinion that the President has the power to issue instructions that there be incorporated in all government contracts for the purchase of supplies a provision requiring that the contractor shall comply with all the terms of the applicable code or agreement.[22]

In an earlier official ruling a Comptroller General held that in the absence of proved violations of a code it is to be presumed that all members of an industry or a trade for which a code has been approved will comply

[22] Opinion of July 29, 1933, 104 CCH 7122.

with its provisions. The mere fact that any member has not pledged compliance should not preclude the awarding of a contract to such member, if he is the lowest bidder otherwise acceptable.[23]

In Pennsylvania it has been ruled that concerns which have not complied with the NRA need not be invited to bid on government contracts.[24]

The statute prescribes the mode of enforcing codes of fair competition and specifies the penalties for the violation of codes. Under elementary principles of law these modes and penalties are exclusive and no others can be legally applied by the goverment.[25] This principle may be of vital importance in dealing with the legality of the limitation of bidders with respect to government contracts. The most important controversy involving this phase of the Recovery Act is that of the Ford Company and the government.

The same principle of the implied exclusion of penalties not expressed in the Act would seem to apply to the boycott under the Blue Eagle as conducted by the government. The refusal to display a Blue Eagle under the rules of the NRA might result in irreparable damage to an enterprise. Such a planned government boycott is openly avowed in connection with the new "Code Blue Eagle." The new emblem will carry an identification of the code under which the company is enrolled and the serial number assigned the individual or firm and this will be issued only to those who have affirmatively pledged compliance with their code. A campaign will be aggressively carried on under the direction of the

[23] Comptroller General Opinions, No. A51737, Nov. 10, 1933, 104 CCH 7073; No. A47742, Nov. 8, 1933, 7074.

[24] Opinion of Attorney General of Pennsylvania, Dec. 29, 1933, 104 CCH 10,190.

[25] 25 Corpus Juris, 1151, and cases there cited.

NRA to convince the public that code compliance symbolized by the display of the Code Blue Eagle should be supported. This form of enforcement is probably the most effective means adopted by the government.

The validity of all indirect methods of enforcement will no doubt be questioned for the reason that Congress, by specifying penalties for the violation of codes and the methods of procedure to enforce obedience, has, by implication, excluded all other penalties and methods. The creation of new penalties for the violation of a statute, or the violation of a code adopted in pursuance of a statute, is a legislative and not an administrative function. The footnote below lists some more or less relevant judicial citations.[26]

Another grave question in the enforcement of codes involves the right of the NRA to compel dealers and manufacturers to furnish complete information as to their private business affairs. The statute authorizing codes provides that "the President may, as a condition of his approval of any such code, impose such conditions (including requirements for the making of reports and the keeping of accounts) for the protection of consumers, competitors, employees, and others." Under the statute the NRA has promulgated broad and sweeping regulations and provisions of codes requiring the furnishing of any and all information which the NRA may deem necessary for the administration of a code. There is no limitation in many codes as to the nature of the information as to a private business which is to be exacted.

[26] (United States): *U. S.* v. *Craft,* 43 Fed. 374.
U. S. v. *Moore,* 43 Fed. 248.
(California): *People* v. *Craycroft,* 2 Calif. 243.
(Missouri): *State* v. *Corwin,* 4 Mo. 609.
(New York): *People* v. *Hislop,* 77 N. Y. 331.
(So. Carolina): *State* v. *Helfrid,* 11 S.C.L. 233.
(Tennessee): *State* v. *Maze,* 6 Humphr. 17.
(Texas): *Phillips* v. *State,* 19 Tex. 158.

Heretofore this power to exact full disclosure of the facts of a business has been confined to those affected with a public interest such as public utilities and railroads. Complete disclosure can now be demanded as to every trade and business.

The right of privacy of personal business affairs, heretofore deemed sacred under the law, will come in sharp conflict with the administration of the Recovery Act. If the NRA can exact any information it may deem necessary for the administration of a code, then the constitutional right of privacy no longer exists. It is annulled on the theory that there is now no private business; but all business has assumed a direct relation to economic security and public welfare and is subject to regulation, and proper and intelligent regulation requires a complete understanding of all of the facts and conditions with respect to the business.

Decisions which have arisen under other federal statutes are of importance in dealing with this question of the inquisitorial power of the government over the most intimate and personal business affairs of the citizen.

In a case involving Section 6 of the Federal Trade Commission Act, it was held that if such section is construed to empower the Commission to examine the books, papers and correspondence of every corporation which does an interstate commerce business whenever the Commission thinks best to make inquiry, it goes beyond any power which Congress can confer.[27]

Again the same statute was construed by the Supreme Court with a strong intimation that if Congress intended to delegate to the Commission under the Commerce Clause such visitorial powers over private corporations

[27] *Federal Trade Commission* v. *Baltimore Grain Co.*, 284 Fed. 886, affirmed 267 U. S. 586.

engaged in interstate commerce as would justify unrestricted inspection of the books, records, and papers of the corporation, with the right to copy therefrom, without some basis of fact tending to establish a charge of wrong-doing, there would be grave doubt of its constitutionality under the Fourth Amendment. The court, however, construed the section as not conferring such power.[28]

The applicable provision of the Fourth Amendment to the Constitution, to which the Supreme Court refers, reads as follows:

"The right of the people to be secure in their persons, houses, papers and effects against unreasonable searches and seizures shall not be violated."

The Fourth Amendment further declares that no person "shall be compelled in any criminal case to be a witness against himself."

The Supreme Court has many times affirmed that the rights assured by the Fourth Amendment are among the dearest of American citizenship. Its deep earnestness is revealed by the following quotation:

"We said in Boyd v. United States, 116 U. S. 616, 630—and it cannot be too often repeated—that the principles that embody the essence of constitutional liberty and security forbid all invasions on the part of the government and its employees of the sanctity of a man's house and the privacies of his life. As said by Mr. Justice Field in *In re* Pacific Ry. Commission, 32 Fed. 241, 250, 'of all the rights of the citizen, few are of greater importance or more essential to his peace and happiness than the right of personal security, and that involves not merely protection of his person from assault, but exemption from the inspection and scrutiny of others. Without the enjoyment of this right, all others would lose half their value.'"[28a]

[28] *Federal Trade Commission* v. *American Tobacco Co.,* 264 U. S. 298.
[28a] *Interstate Commerce Commission* v. *Brimson,* 154 U. S. 447.

These questions to which I have alluded are perhaps but a few of the many legal and constitutional problems that will arise in the application and enforcement of codes. I have touched on matters in a paragraph or sentence that could well be the subject of an entire chapter or even of a volume. The new legislation opens a limitless field for inquiry in the application of basic law. It will be extremely difficult to work out solutions with the old tools of precedents and analogies.

The national government, recognizing the magnitude of the task of code enforcement, as well as the doubtful validity of codes when applied to strictly local activities, has been seeking coöperative legislation from the various states. We have seen that this action was in the mind of the Congress when it enacted the law. The Recovery Act gives the President the power to utilize, with the consent of the states, all state and local officers in carrying out the provisions of the statute.[29] As early as June, 1933, the NRA announced to the states its "interest in the passage of state legislation providing for state coöperation with the NRA and the elimination of any conflicts in the carrying out of the purpose and policy of the National Industrial Recovery Act which might arise by virtue of existing state laws."[30] In furtherance of the scheme of dovetailing national and state legislation and enforcement, the NRA prepared a proposed model state act sent to all state governors "to encourage state and national industrial recovery by coöperating with the national government in fostering fair competition."[31] Twenty-three states have now either adopted this model law or have enacted measures for coöperation in the en-

[29] NIRA, Section 2 (a).

[30] NRA Official Releases No. 7, June 22, 1933, and No. 27, July 5, 1933.

[31] The first draft of the act was sent in August, 1933, but was not made public. The proposed act was made public on February 12, 1934.

forcement of the Recovery Act. There is great dissimilarity in these state enactments. Some of them provide for state codes. Others provide for the filing of national codes with the Secretary of State giving the code *ipso facto* the force of state law. Other state enactments have changed the labor provisions of the Recovery Act. Inevitably grave conflicts must arise in the administration of the federal and state legislation.

The enactment of local laws is, of course, unnecessary to make the NIRA effective in every state in the Union and binding upon every inhabitant so far as its provisions are within the power of Congress and not in contravention of the restraints of the Federal Constitution. Local statutes are of value as auxiliary enforcement procedure and in removing doubt as to the application of the Recovery Act to strictly local transactions. The complete national operation of the Recovery Act and its essential force as adopted by Congress, directly obligatory on every citizen, proceeds from this section of the Federal Constitution:

> "This constitution and the laws of the United States which shall be made in pursuance thereof, and all treaties made, or which shall be made under the authority of the United States, shall be the supreme law of the land; and the judges in every state shall be bound thereby; anything in the constitution or laws of any state to the contrary notwithstanding."[32]

Seven words of that paragraph — "which shall be made in pursuance thereof" — were weighted with destiny. By implication they created the power in the Supreme Court to declare void an act of Congress. They have supplied the theme for historic drama. These seven words have

[32] Constitution of the United States, Article VI, Sec. 1.

profoundly affected the social and industrial evolution of America. Only laws made in pursuance of the Constitution are the supreme law of the land. All the codes and decrees and penalties we have been discussing, this discursive review of the Recovery Act and its creature the NRA, will be as sounding brass and tinkling cymbal unless the statute meets this ultimate test: Is it a law made in pursuance of the Constitution?

CHAPTER VII

THE CONSTITUTION IN AN ECONOMIC EMERGENCY

THE Supreme Court has not considered the Recovery Act as a whole, or any of its provisions. NRA works steadily on, drawing under its power all the trade and business of the country, with its basic constitutional validity undetermined and, in the opinion of respected authority, gravely in doubt. Ninety-five per cent of the business of the country is under codes. Over 400 more codes are in process of formation. The Act creating the NRA expires, according to its terms, on June 16, 1935. This Cyclops of bureaucracy may exert its powers to the end and slip into its predestined grave before the question of its lawful birth is authoritatively determined. The Supreme Court will continue to sit in cold neutrality until a litigated case directly involving the constitutional issue comes within its jurisdiction. With that court silent "the merest hint of dogmatic certainty as to finality of statement," to borrow an apt observation, "is an exhibition of folly."

If the constitutional problems involved in the Recovery Act come before the Supreme Court for solution, no precedents will in reality control its decision. The doctrine of the binding effect of precedent is of little weight in that court in dealing with great constitutional questions, and is not inflexible in other cases. The Court has in a number of instances overruled its own definite and deliberate decisions when precisely the same question has again been presented. Whether or not the rule of *stare decisis* will be followed in the Supreme Court is obviously a matter resting within its discretion. Mr. Justice Cardozo has written:

> "I think that when a rule, after it has been duly tested by experience, has been found to be inconsistent with the sense of justice or with the social welfare, there should be less hesitation in frank avowal and full abandonment."[1]

Great constitutional questions are always open. Definitions of today may be obsolete tomorrow. Limitations on power imposed in one decision may yield under new and unforeseen conditions requiring a larger exercise of power. "The Constitution," says Judge Manton, "is what the judges say it is, and the Supreme Court is the ultimate tribunal."[2] A noted historian has written:

> "To the decision of an underlying question of constitutional law . . . no finality attaches. To endure, it must be right."[3]

What the Constitution is with respect to the NRA will be what the present Supreme Court says is the Constitution with respect to the NRA. The fate of the great experiment rests with those nine grave men, or five of them, with their individual characteristics, their legal training, respect for prior decisions, economic and social background, their insight, grasp and appreciation of the economic crisis and their individual conceptions of what a constitution really is and should mean.

The Supreme Court may not, as Mr. Dooley said, follow the election returns, but there is no doubt what-

[1] *The Nature of the Judicial Process,* p. 150.
[2] Manton, "Historical Fragments Pertaining to the United States Supreme Court," N. Y. L. J. – Sept. 28, 1932, page 1173.
[3] "Works of George Bancroft," quoted in Warren, *The Supreme Court,* Vol. 3, p. 471.

soever that it is responsive to the temper of the people, and in its judgment a constitutional decision to be right must be consonant with the spirit of the times. There is also no doubt that the Supreme Court in dealing with legislation considers whether or not it is of real benefit to the country.

Recent decisions and accepted legal philosophy emphasize the living and adaptable nature of the Constitution. It is a living document made for a changing society with provisions that must adapt themselves to changing conditions and changing needs. Fundamentally it exists for human welfare and its protection and promotion under ever-changing conditions. "When we are dealing with words that also are a constituent act like the Constitution of the United States," said the Supreme Court, "we must realize that they have called into life a being, the development of which could not have been foreseen completely by the most gifted of its begetters. . . The case before us must be considered in the light of our whole experience and not merely in that of what was said a hundred years ago."[3a] Chief Justice Marshall uttered this memorable warning against narrow and too legalistic reasoning:

> "We must never forget that it is a constitution we are expounding . . . a constitution intended to endure for ages to come, and, consequently be adapted to the various crises of human affairs."[4]

And in the very recent case, the Minnesota Mortgage Moratorium case,[5] the Supreme Court again reiterated that it is not sound interpretation that the great clauses of the Constitution must be confined to the meaning

[3a] *Missouri* v. *Holland,* 252 U. S. 416, 433.
[4] *McCulloch* v. *Maryland,* 4 Wheat. (U. S.) 316, 407 (1819).
[5] *Home Building & Loan Assn.* v. *Blaisdell,* 290 U. S. 422 (1933).

which the framers, with the conditions and outlook of their time, would have placed upon them, but they must be interpreted under present conditions and adapted today to the needs of the people.

Chief Justice Hughes in this very recent opinion stated:

"It is manifest from this review of our decisions that there has been a growing appreciation of public needs and of the necessity of finding ground for a rational compromise between individual rights and public welfare. The settlement and consequent contraction of the public domain, the pressure of a constantly increasing density of population, the interrelation of the activities of our people and the complexity of our economic interest, have inevitably led to an increased use of the organization of society in order to protect the very bases of individual opportunity. Where, in earlier days, it was thought that only the concerns of individuals or of classes were involved, and that those of the State itself were touched only remotely, it has later been found that the fundamental interests of the State are directly affected; and that the question is no longer merely that of one party to a contract as against another, but of the use of reasonable means to safeguard the economic structure upon which the good of all depends."

By this language the Chief Justice has made it clear that the present judicial conception of the Constitution is that it is a living instrument and must be construed in the light of ever-changing conditions and adapted to human needs and human life which are not static but ever moving. Constitutional development is a continuous process which has not ended. Its essence is an evolutionary process adapting basic law under the impact of a changing civilization to new and unprecedented conditions and problems.

Sixty-two years ago the author of a book dealing

with the Federal Constitution wrote in his preface this observation:

"The difference between a community of three millions of people, scattered along a narrow belt of sea-coast, inclosed by impenetrable forests; and thirty or forty millions, occupying half a continent, and pursuing all the objects, and by all the arts and means, which the reason or passions, the interest or ambition, the virtues or vices, of men could invent,—must soon make itself apparent in the inevitable development of those powers of regulation which were expressly designed and intended to provide for just such increasing claims for their exercise."[6]

The writer of that paragraph did not know the telephone, motor car, airplane, radio or gasoline engine; nor the colossal aggregations of capital by the consolidation and interlocking of corporations; nor the giant public utilities or oil companies; nor trade unionism in the form of national combinations of workers. What would be his state of mind if he beheld the scene today, the intricate social system in which 120,000,000 human beings are enmeshed? The same Constitution at which he marveled still governs. "The Government, within the Constitution, has all the powers granted to it which are necessary to preserve its existence."[7] "Our Constitution," said President Roosevelt in his inaugural address, "is so simple and practical that it is possible always to meet extraordinary needs by changes in emphasis and arrangement without loss of essential form."

The work of the Supreme Court of the United States in the past one hundred and fifty years has been in the extension of federal constitutional power rather than its restriction. Will this trend in constitutional expansion

[6] *Manual of the Constitution,* Timothy Farrar (1872).
[7] Ex Parte *Milligan,* 4 Wall. (U. S.), 2, 121 (1866).

of federal power go one step further and uphold the validity of the new and extraordinary exercises of power found in the National Industrial Recovery Act?

There is always a presumption that an act of Congress is constitutional. "A decent respect for a coördinate branch of the government demands that the judiciary shall presume, until the contrary is clearly shown, that there has been no transgression of power by Congress."[8] This presumption of validity, while persuasive, has been frequently overcome and the Supreme Court, in at least sixty cases, has held that laws enacted by Congress were beyond its power or, if within a granted power, were in contravention of a constitutional limitation.[8a] The Supreme Court cannot declare a statute unconstitutional because it deems the means employed by Congress in the discharge of its powers to be inexpedient or unwise. Congress has a wide discretion as to the means or methods to be used in the execution of a granted power. To render a law unconstitutional it must plainly transcend the granted power or plainly contravene a limitation in the Constitution on the exercise of power.

A great judge spoke as follows:

> "There is great danger, it seems to me, to arise from the constant habit which prevails where anything is opposed or objected to, of resorting without rhyme or reason to the Constitution as a means of preventing its accomplishment, thus creating the general impression that the Constitution is but a barrier to progress instead of being the broad highway through which alone true progress may be enjoyed."[9]

A grave financial crisis and economic emergency of

[8] *Knox* v. *Lee* (Legal Tender Cases), 12 Wall. (U. S.), 457, 531 (1870).

[8a] See "New Deal and the Constitution" by Albert Russell Ellingwood, *Illinois Law Review,* Feb., 1934, p. 731.

[9] Quoted from address of Chief Justice White before the American Bar Association in 1914.

unparalleled magnitude and severity, threatening the whole industrial structure, existed at the time of the passage of the Recovery Act. Does this fact affect its constitutional validity? I believe we can answer this question in the affirmative, without subscribing to the theory that the Constitution is one thing during an emergency and something different during more normal times. That the Constitution is not changed under the impact of a crisis was forcefully stated many years ago by the Supreme Court in these words:

> "The Constitution of the United States is a law for rulers and people, equally in war and in peace, and covers with the shield of its protection all classes of men, at all times, and under all circumstances. No doctrine, involving more pernicious consequences, was ever invented by the wit of man than that any of its provisions can be suspended during any of the great exigencies of government."[10]

The Recovery Act is emergency legislation. It expires within two years from the date of its passage or sooner if the President or Congress declares the emergency ended. The law was framed under the impelling pressure of a crisis. "A national emergency," the Act declares, "productive of widespread unemployment and disorganization of industry, which burdens interstate and foreign commerce, affects the public welfare, and undermines the standards of living of the American people, is hereby declared to exist." Closed banks, idle plants, prostrate credit, stranded industry, disappearing trade, widespread unemployment producing want and distress and almost despair were the conditions under which the statute was framed and adopted. These conditions affected the minds and hearts of all men. They dictated

[10] Ex Parte *Milligan,* 4 Wall. (U. S.), 2, 120 (1866).

policies and determined decisions. They created the critical problems with which Congress was faced and which it had the grave responsibility to meet. In the light of such conditions, such concrete facts, and the then actual impelling problems, the Recovery Act must be studied and tested.

The Recovery Act was a part of a legislative program for recovery from a great depression, a program which was not "just a collection of haphazard schemes, but rather the orderly component parts of a connected logical whole."[11]

The objectives and provisions of the Recovery Act were designed to save the financial and economic structure. Its declared purposes were to remove obstructions to the free flow of commerce and which tended to diminish the amount thereof; to promote the general welfare by the organization of industry for coöperative action; to induce united action of labor and management under adequate governmental sanction and supervision; to eliminate unfair competitive practices; to promote the fullest possible utilization of the present productive capacity of industries; to avoid undue restrictions of production (except as may be temporarily required); to increase the consumption of industrial and agricultural products by increasing purchasing power; to reduce and relieve unemployment; to improve standards of labor, and otherwise to rehabilitate industry and to conserve natural resources.

The realization of these objectives was the purpose of the Act and its whole scheme for the control of trade and industry under codes must be judged in the light of the emergency, the purposes of the statute, and the means

[11] Quoted from an address of President Roosevelt. See "The New Deal and the Constitution," Albert Russell Ellingwood, *Illinois Law Review* for February, 1934, page 730.

and methods employed by Congress to fulfill such purposes.

In the notable dissenting opinion of Mr. Justice Brandeis written in the Oklahoma Ice case[12] he wrote:

"The people of the United States are now confronted with an emergency more serious than war. Misery is wide-spread, in a time, not of scarcity, but of over-abundance. The long-continued depression has brought unprecedented unemployment, a catastrophic fall in commodity prices and a volume of economic losses which threatens our financial institutions. Some people believe that the existing conditions threaten even the stability of the capitalistic system. . . There must be power in the States and the Nation to remould, through experimentation, our economic practices and institutions to meet changing social and economic needs. . . To stay experimentation in things social and economic is a grave responsibility. Denial of the right to experiment may be fraught with serious consequences to the Nation. . . This Court has the power to prevent an experiment. . . But in the exercise of this high power, we must be ever on our guard, lest we erect our prejudices into legal principles. If we would guide by the light of reason, we must let our minds be bold."

The existence of a financial crisis or economic emergency has in a number of important instances, in the opinion of the Supreme Court, justified an extraordinary and unprecedented exercise of powers for the protection of the public welfare. Statutes regulating rents by prohibiting excessive increases, an aftermath of the War, were in 1921 held valid. These statutes were a wholly novel exercise of the power of our government and were designed to protect citizens from injustice and oppression during an emergency. The District of Columbia rent statute was limited to two years and provided that tenants

[12] *New State Ice Company* v. *Liebmann,* 285 U. S. 262, 306-311 (1931).

might remain beyond the expiration of their leases at the same rental, except as changed by a commission. The statute was upheld by the Supreme Court on the ground that "the circumstances have clothed the letting of buildings in the District of Columbia with a public interest so great as to justify regulation by law," and that "a limit in time to tide over a passing trouble may justify a law that could not be upheld as a permanent change."[13] In upholding one of these statutes, the Supreme Court through Mr. Justice Holmes stated:

"Plainly circumstances may so change in time or so differ in space as to clothe with such an (*i.e.* a public) interest what at other times or in other places would be a matter of purely private concern."[14]

In a later case involving a similar law, the Court, through the same Justice, uttered this doctrine:

"A law depending upon the existence of an emergency or other certain state of facts to uphold it may cease to operate if the emergency ceases or the facts change, even though valid when passed."

General rules must yield to exceptional circumstances. In *Wilson* v. *New,* the famous Adamson Law case, an act of Congress was upheld which, in view of probable irreparable injury through the paralysis of the nation's commerce by threatened nationwide strike of railway employees, fixed their hours of service and their wages for a period sufficient to permit a general investigation of their complaints.[15]

In the latter case Mr. Chief Justice White stated:

"Although an emergency may not call into life a power which has never lived, nevertheless emergency may afford a

[13] *Block* v. *Hirsch* (1921), 256 U. S. 135; *Marcus Brown Holding Co.* v. *Feldman* (1921), 256 U. S. 170.
[14] *Block* v. *Hirsch,* supra.
[15] 243 U. S. 332 (1917).

reason for the exertion of a living power already enjoyed . . ."

In the Adamson case there was a strong dissent by Justice Pitney. He declared:

"The suggestion that it [the Act regulating hours and wages of trainmen] was passed to prevent a threatened strike, and in this sense to remove an obstruction from the path of commerce, while true in fact is immaterial in law. It amounts to no more than saying that it was enacted to take care of an emergency. But an emergency can neither create power, nor excuse a defiance of the limitations upon the powers of the Government."

In a later case the Supreme Court by unanimous opinion held that the action of the President in fixing the prices of coal during the War under the Lever Act and the enactment of the statue itself were not unreasonable or arbitrary exercises of power.[16]

In its very recent decision (Minnesota Mortgage Moratorium case) the Supreme Court in its opinion uses this language:

"Emergency does not create power. Emergency does not increase granted power or remove or diminish the restrictions imposed upon power granted or reserved."

A grave emergency requires emergency legislation. Extraordinary evils demand extraordinary remedies. A national crisis may require original and bold and drastic measures and methods to save the economic system from deeper chaos, if not destruction. Unheard of exercises of powers may be necessary. But the question remains: Are these measures within a power actually granted to Congress? Has Congress transcended

[16] *Highland* v. *Russell Car & Snow Plow Co.*, 279 U. S. 253.

any constitutional restrictions on its exercise of power? If so, the measures are void if we have a government constituted by, functioning within, and restrained by, a constitution.

From all that has been said and decided, the sound deduction is that an emergency does not create or expand power. Its only relevancy is in determining the reasonableness of the exercise of power under the existing state of facts. The powers of Congress in a crisis are those stated in the Constitution.

By an emergency power is not created, but the reasonableness of the exercise of power must be tested by the conditions under which the law was enacted and the evils which it was intended to remove. The legislation must be addressed to a legitimate end and the measures taken must be reasonable and appropriate to that end. Proponents of the constitutionality of the Recovery Act will vividly describe the emergency and by reasoning similar to that of Justice Brandeis will assert that the Act was a reasonable and appropriate exercise of power. The consideration of the nature of the emergency and the character of the measures necessary to meet it manifestly involve questions of fact.

It is perfectly clear that the existence of an emergency does not clothe the government with arbitrary power. It does not vest in Congress a supreme unlimited power to legislate for the public welfare. The reasonableness and necessity of all legislative remedies for a depression must be reviewed and passed upon by the courts. If regulations of business and restrictions on freedom of action of the citizen are arbitrary or unreasonable, if they are not in fact required by actual conditions or public necessity, they will be held an invalid exercise of power and annulled. The doctrine may be illustrated by a number of recent cases. One is the *Nebbia* case. The gist of that decision was the validation of the law of New York under which Nebbia was convicted for selling milk at less than nine cents a quart in violation of the order of the Milk Control Board made in the exercise of statutory authority. The statute professedly was aimed at the existence of certain evils. The regulation of the dairy business was upheld, the court saying:

"In the light of the facts the order appears not to be unreasonable or arbitrary, or without relation to the purpose to prevent ruthless competition from destroying the wholesale price structure on which the farmer depends for his livelihood, and the community for an assured supply of milk."

Powerful dissenting opinions were rendered in the *Nebbia* case, warning against "facile disregard of the Constitution as long interpreted and respected" and containing cogent arguments against the appropriateness of this particular New York statute as a means of improving the condition of the milk industry.[17]

Contrasted with that decision is one of the same court dealing with the action of the Governor of Texas in declaring martial law and suspending the production of oil.[18] It was held that whether or not an exigency existed justifying such interference with the rights of the citizen was not settled by the acts or declarations of the Governor but was subject to judicial inquiry and determination. The court found that no such exigency existed as validated the government action.

That constitutional limitations annul legislative action taken during an emergency and for the supposed welfare

[17] *People* v. *Nebbia,* 54 Sup. Ct. 505 (1933).
[18] *Sterling* v. *Constantin,* 287 U. S. 378 (1933).

of the people is again illustrated by a decision announced by the Supreme Court while these pages are being written.[19] The court ruled invalid the statute of Arkansas which exempted proceeds of insurance policies from legal seizure for debts.[20] The statute was without limitation as to time, amount, circumstances, or need. It was held an extreme and unreasonable and arbitrary exercise of legislative power. This conclusion seems incontrovertibly sound, but it has little application to the Recovery Act.

The recent decisions validating state statutes, including the New York Milk Act, attacked under the Due Process Clause in the Fourteenth Amendment, and the drastic decision upholding the Minnesota statute giving the courts the power to extend the time for redemption from mortgages, attacked upon the ground that it impaired the obligation of contracts, deal with emergency measures of the states under their general police power and have no direct relation to the Recovery Act. The general police power applies to the states and was never delegated to the national government. It originally and always belonged to them. Unlike state legislatures, Congress has only granted powers. It possesses only the powers enumerated in the Constitution. It may enact measures for the general welfare in the execution of its enumerated powers. In that respect it may be said to have a qualified or limited police power. No general police

[19] *Worthen Company* v. *Thomas*, 291 U. S. — (1934).

[20] The statute reads:

"All moneys paid or payable to any resident of this state as the insured or beneficiary designated under any insurance policy or policies providing for the payment of life, sick, accident and/or disability benefits shall be exempt from liability or seizure under judicial process of any court, and shall not be subjected to the payment of any debt by contract or otherwise by any writ, order, judgment, or decree of any court, provided, that the validity of any sale, assignment, mortgage, pledge or hypothecation of any policy of insurance, or if any avails, proceeds or benefits thereof, now made, or hereafter made, shall in no way be affected by the provisions of this act."

power in the Federal Government is created by an emergency.[21]

Even if an emergency justifies novel and drastic regulations of trade and industry it does not follow that all business can lawfully be subjected to the same regulations. "A regulation valid for one kind of business may, of course, be invalid for another; since the reasonableness of every regulation is dependent upon the relevant facts . . . the state's power extends to every regulation of any business reasonably required and appropriate for the public protection." [22]

Applying the criteria of recent decisions of the Supreme Court, we conclude that new and extraordinary exercises of power during a financial crisis, or economic emergency, may be deemed valid, although such exercises of power under more normal conditions would be considered unreasonable and arbitrary. Certain commercial and industrial practices may be considered injurious to public interests during an emergency, which during other times would be harmless and not subject to government regulations. Conduct may be considered inequitable and oppressive under emergency conditions

21 In dealing with the wartime Prohibition Act, and upholding its constitutionality, the Supreme Court (*Hamilton* v. *Kentucky Distilleries Co.*, 251 U. S. 146 (1919) made this statement:

"That the United States lacks the police power, and that this was reserved to the States by the Tenth Amendment, is true. But it is none the less true that when the United States exerts any of the powers conferred upon it by the Constitution, no valid objection can be based upon the fact that such exercise may be attended by the same incidents which attend the exercise by a State of its police power, or that it may tend to accomplish a similar purpose. Lottery case, 188 U. S. 321, 357; *McCray* v. *United States*, 195 U. S. 27; *Hipolite Egg Co.* v. *United States*, 220 U. S. 45, 58; *Hoke* v. *United States*, 227 U. S. 308, 323; *Seven Cases* v. *United States*, 239 U. S. 510, 515; *United States* v. *Doremus*, 249 U. S. 86, 93, 94."

An authoritative writer, Ernst Freund, in his book, *"The Police Power,"* Par. 65, states:

"The Federal exercise of the police power through positive regulation rests upon the enumerated powers of Congress under the Constitution."

22 Mr. Justice Brandeis' dissenting opinion, *New State Ice Co.* v. *Liebmann*, 285 U. S. 262, 301-303 (1932).

which would be proper under different conditions. Means and methods for the regulation of commerce may be employed by Congress to meet an emergency, which at other times would be held to infringe upon constitutional inhibitions.

But nevertheless the Constitution is essentially unchanged. Restraints on legislative and executive action are not suspended by any exigencies of government. No emergency justifies the denial or curtailment of liberty or the destruction of property by measures that are unreasonable or arbitrary. Whatever the crisis, the Constitution "covers with the shield of its protection all classes of men, at all times, and under all circumstances."[23]

"The Constitution," declared the Supreme Court in a very recent decision, "was adopted in a period of grave emergency. Its grants of power to the Federal Government and its limitations of the power of the States were determined in the light of emergency and they are not altered by emergency. What power was thus granted and what limitations were thus imposed are questions which have always been, and always will be, the subject of close examination under our constitutional system."

The precise constitutional questions during an emergency are whether the power is actually possessed and whether such power embraces the particular exercise of it in response to particular conditions.[24] During an emergency, as in more normal periods, the Federal Constitution remains, as stated by Mr. Justice Story, "the frame of a national government, of *special* and *enumerated* powers, and not of general and unlimited powers."

Two things are of the very essence of this frame of

[23] Ex Parte *Milligan,* 4 Wall. (U. S.), 2, 120.
[24] *Home Building & Loan Assn.* v. *Blaisdell,* 290 U. S. 398, at 425.

government. One is the dual structure of the government: states and a union of states. The other is the separation and delimitation of powers between the legislative, executive and judicial departments. Equally fundamental is the constitutional restraint which applies to all federal legislative, executive and administrative action, that no man can be deprived of life, liberty or property without due process of law.

Applying these fundamental truths to the National Industrial Recovery Act, viewing the constitutionality of that Act as a whole, three constitutional problems arise:

Does the Recovery Act fall within one of the special and enumerated powers of Congress?

Are there in the Act provisions which in their operation necessarily involve a deprivation of life, liberty or property of the citizen without due process of law?

Is the Recovery Act in its delegation of powers to the President in harmony with the essential nature of the structure of the government?

CHAPTER VIII

THE COMMERCE CLAUSE AS A BASIS OF POWER

THE draughtsmen and sponsors of the Act professed to find authority for its enactment from three constitutional sources:

The Preamble of the Constitution;
The General Welfare Clause;
The Commerce Clause.

The preamble of the Constitution uses the words "general welfare" and from this it has been argued by rather fantastic reasoning that the framers of the Constitution intended to vest in Congress supreme and unlimited power to legislate for the general welfare. It is, however, settled that the preamble of the Constitution confers no power on Congress. Mr. Justice Story, in his classic work on the Constitution, said:

"The preamble never can be resorted to to enlarge the powers confined to the general government or any of its departments. It cannot confer any power *per se;* it can never amount, by implication, to an enlargement of any power expressly given."

This rule has been accepted by the courts, and the Supreme Court has definitely declared that "although that preamble indicates the general purposes for which the people ordained and established the Constitution, it has never been regarded as the source of any substantive power conferred on the government of the United States or on any of its departments."[1]

The second source of constitutional authority cited to

[1] *Jacobson* v. *Massachusetts,* 197 U. S. 11, 22.

support the Recovery Act is the general welfare clause found in Section 8 of Article I dealing with the power to lay taxes.[2]

This language, it has been authoritatively determined, does not confer a general legislative power. The exposition of this part of the Constitution by Mr. Justice Story has been accepted as final. He made it plain that the words "general welfare" as used in this section must be construed to be connected with the power to lay taxes, duties, imposts and excises, so as "to constitute a qualification upon them," and that they are not to be interpreted to extend to any other power. If these words, "for the common defense and general welfare," refer to a distinct and substantial power other than that to lay and collect taxes, then "it is obvious that, under color of the generality of the words 'to provide for the common defense and general welfare,' the government of the United States is, in reality, a government of general and unlimited powers, notwithstanding the subsequent enumeration of specific powers." The general welfare clause contains no grant of power, but it is a mere expression of the ends and purposes to be effected by the power of taxation.[3]

The third source of constitutional power claimed for the Recovery Act, *i.e.*, the commerce clause of the Constitution, remains as the only express grant of power to Congress upon which it may, with any reason, be contended that the Act can be sustained.

Section 8, paragraph 3, of Article I, dealing with the powers of Congress reads:

[2] That section reads: "The Congress shall have the power to lay and collect Taxes, Duties, Imposts and Excises, to pay the Debts and provide for the common Defense and general welfare of the United States; but all Duties, Imposts and Excises shall be uniform throughout the United States."

[3] Story, *Commentaries on the Constitution*, 4th Ed., Vol. 2, Chapter XIV.

"To regulate commerce with foreign nations, and among the several states and with the Indian tribes."

The definition and application of the meaning and scope of this clause of the Federal Constitution has been the great task of the Supreme Court for over a century. It has been given a construction broad and comprehensive, adapted to ever-changing conditions and developments. "To regulate," under the decisions, is a very broad phrase. It means "to foster, protect, control and restrain, with appropriate regard for those who are immediately concerned and for the public at large." The power to regulate commerce has been expanded to apply to a great variety of regulatory measures since the decision of Chief Justice Marshall, expressing his conception of the nature and scope of the power. This was in the case of *Gibbons* v. *Ogden*.[4] The opinion of Marshall in this case is universally conceded to be one of the great products of his profound and luminous intellect. It contains an exhaustive discussion of the subject of commerce and its regulation by Congress in all its bearings and aspects and under all conditions, and has furnished the principles for the guidance of the courts in the numberless and diverse cases down to the present time. By that decision commerce was made forever free from state interference and placed under the plenary protection of the Federal Government. The precise point decided was that navigation was a part of commerce and no state could impose upon navigation a regulation which would interfere with or tend to annul the Act of Congress. Interstate commerce, then concretely the business of a small steamboat plying the Hudson and carrying package freight between points in New

[4] 9 Wheat. (U. S.) 1 (1824). For a dramatic account of this case see the *Life of John Marshall*, by Albert J. Beveridge, Vol. IV, p. 397.

York and New Jersey, developed over the century into the interstate commerce of railroads, telegraph, telephone, motor vehicles, aviation and radio, a vast and highly complicated financial, commercial and industrial system, yet the principles announced by John Marshall in 1824 still govern it.

The conception of commerce as essentially national was voiced by Chief Justice Taft in a decision several years ago, as follows:

"Commerce is a unit and does not regard state lines, and while, under the Constitution, interstate and intrastate commerce are ordinarily subject to regulation by different sovereignties, yet when they are so mingled together that the supreme authority, the Nation, cannot exercise complete effective control over interstate commerce without incidental regulation of intrastate commerce, such incidental regulation is not an invasion of state authority or a violation of the proviso."

Commerce means intercourse by way of trade and traffic. It includes commercial intercourse in all its branches. No limitation has been placed upon these words of the Constitution. They are broad enough to permit the exercise of authority to keep pace with progress and development, not only of commercial intercourse, but with all the means and methods employed in that intercourse. "Under modern conditions," said Chief Justice Taft, "commerce is a continuous flow from production through the various stages of distribution until the consumer is reached. Touch this flow at any point and you affect the commerce itself." [5]

There can be no doubt from the language of the Recovery Act that its framers intended to base its constitutional validity on the Commerce Clause. Section 1 of Title I of the Act reads:

[5] *Stafford* v. *Wallace*, 258 U. S. 495.

"It is hereby declared to be the policy of Congress to remove obstructions to the free flow of interstate and foreign commerce which tend to diminish the amount thereof."

In the same section of the statute the national emergency is declared to be one "which burdens interstate and foreign commerce." Manifestly the primary intent of the Congress was to legislate with regard to evils, interferences and obstructions affecting the free flow of interstate and foreign commerce and for the removal of conditions which placed a burden on interstate and foreign commerce or tended to diminish the amount thereof.

Again in dealing with codes, the law [Section 3 (*b*)] provides "any violation of such standards in any transaction *in or affecting* interstate or foreign commerce shall be deemed an unfair method of competition in commerce within the meaning of the Federal Trade Commission Act, as amended."

Section 4, paragraph (b), in dealing with the licensing power of the President, provides that such license shall be a condition to the right to "engage in or carry on any business in or affecting interstate or foreign commerce."

These references to interstate and foreign commerce running through the statute will be used to support its basic constitutional validity. It will be contended that while the statute in its operation embraces all trade and industry in the country, it constitutionally so operates because at the time of its enactment in the existing crisis and at the time of its application all business either involved or affected interstate commerce.

Attorney General Homer S. Cummings expressed this view in an address before the American Bar Association:

"Today almost every economic and social problem is both local and national. Manufacturing, merchandising, transportation, agriculture, mining, oil production, problems of employment and unemployment, of strikes and the settlement thereof, are upon a national scale, or, if local in scope, are *national in effect.* Child labor in one state may destroy an industry in another."

The determination of the constitutionality of the Recovery Act will require a painstaking and exhaustive study of all the social and economic phenomena involved in the emergency during which the measure was enacted, a close analysis of all of the provisions of the Act itself, a decision as to whether or not the Act is within a granted power of Congress, a decision as to whether the provisions of the Act were at the time of its passage necessary and reasonably designed to regulate commerce and thereby protect and promote the welfare of the people. The objectives of the statute must relate to the removal of interferences and obstructions to the free flow of interstate and foreign commerce, and the provisions of the Act must have a real and substantial relationship to such interferences and obstructions.

It is axiomatic that a statute cannot be broader than the power of the legislative department under which it was enacted.

The view of the administration is that it was necessary for Congress to take jurisdiction over all business under the existing emergency in order to save and safeguard the economic structure upon which the welfare of the country depended. In other words, effectively to foster and protect interstate commerce under then existing conditions it was necessary to control intrastate commerce; or to state it in another way, all business was then affected with a public interest and all business either entered into or affected the flow of interstate commerce, and statutes embracing all trade and industry were therefore under existing conditions a reasonable exercise of the power created by the Commerce Clause.

The Recovery Act does not, it is argued, seek to regulate manufacturing or production or local business as such, but as phenomena that affected interstate commerce in a substantial and real manner. The control of intrastate activities was necessary to relieve interstate commerce from interferences and interruptions and destruction; to release it from burdens; to maintain its free flow throughout the nation. No regulation by the Congress of interstate commerce, it will be argued, would be sufficient or effectual or complete; it would in fact be inadequate and futile, unless under the existing conditions it met the whole emergency and dealt with and embraced within its legislation all the trade and commerce in the country.

There can be no question that this statute, in its necessary effect and direct and immediate operation, applies to business which heretofore has been considered as strictly and exclusively local and intrastate within the province and jurisdiction of the states, and not subject to regulation by Congress. The statute deals with production and manufacture, with hours of work, minimum wages, collective bargaining, and with all other conditions of employment approved or prescribed by the President, and in dealing with such matters it deals universally with every trade or industry. The statute provides for involuntary or compulsory codes governing every trade or business. It provides for mandatory clauses of such codes and one of these mandatory clauses is that employers shall comply with the maximum hours of labor, minimum rates of pay and other conditions of employment approved or prescribed by the President. The statute further provides [Section

6 (*c*)] that where there has been no agreement approved by the President, then the President may "investigate the labor practices, policies, wages, hours of labor, and conditions of employment in such trade or industry or subdivision thereof; and upon the basis of such investigations, and after such hearings as the President finds advisable, he is authorized to prescribe a limited code of fair competition fixing such maximum hours of labor, minimum rates of pay, and other conditions of employment in the trade or industry or subdivision thereof investigated as he finds to be necessary to effectuate the policy of this title, which shall have the same effect as a code of fair competition approved by the President under subsection (a) of Section 3." The President is also given the power under the licensing provisions to prohibit any person from engaging in or carrying on any business in or affecting interstate or foreign commerce.

In its direct and indirect operation the Recovery Act touches all trade and commerce.

The regulation of business, which heretofore has been considered strictly local and intrastate, proceeds under provisions which are not entirely permissible and voluntary, but which under certain circumstances are compulsory and mandatory. While the Act provides for the adoption of voluntary codes which embrace the whole trade and industry of the country, these codes, when approved by the President, are made binding upon every dealer and manufacturer in the industry, even though he did not participate in the formation of the code or accept or assent to its provisions. No member of an industry and no trade association can act as an agent of any dealer or manufacturer, or in any way bind another dealer or manufacturer to a code, unless authorized to so act. As between the President and dissenting members of the industry there is no contract and no voluntary acceptance. The validity and binding effect of the code upon such dealers and manufacturers must be through the force of the statute and the statute will have no force unless it was constitutionally adopted. The same reasoning applies to the compulsory codes authorized by the Act which rest for their validity upon the action of the President under the statute. Furthermore, the statute prescribes certain provisions that are necessary for all codes and which must be incorporated in all codes even against the consent and protest of the industry. It is, therefore, plain that the regulations of trade and industry contained in codes are in effect compulsory federal statutes which are invalid unless within the constitutional power of the Congress to regulate interstate and foreign commerce.

Two lines of prior decisions of the Supreme Court will be cited in dealing with the constitutionality of this Act. The protagonists of constitutionality will cite one line of these decisions; the advocates of invalidity will rest their case upon the other. The prior decisions under which the constitutionality of the Recovery Act will be attacked are those in which the Supreme Court has sharply differentiated between interstate business and local business and has declared that with respect to local or internal business within the state no regulatory measure of Congress can have any validity or operation. The prior decisions of the Supreme Court which will be cited by the advocates of constitutionality are those, mostly recent cases, in which the conception of the commerce clause has been definitely broadened and the regulatory power of Congress construed to extend over all transactions which *affect* or *influence* interstate commerce.

There can be no escape from the conclusion that in

many prior decisions the Supreme Court of the United States has announced doctrines which appear as insuperable obstacles to a present decision holding that the Recovery Act is constitutional. The legal reasoning in such cases must be abandoned if the Recovery Act is to be held valid.

In 1870 the Supreme Court held invalid a federal statute prohibiting the sale, without restriction to interstate transactions, of certain mixtures of naphtha. The Court said that "within state limits it (the law) can have no constitutional operation." In another case [5a] the Supreme Court held that although 80 per cent of Pennsylvania coal is shipped out of the state, mining in Pennsylvania is subject exclusively to state control. A contrary holding, the court stated, "would nationalize and withdraw from state jurisdiction and deliver to federal commercial control the fruits of California and the South, the wheat of the West and its meats, the cotton of the South, the shoes of Massachusetts, and the woolen industries of other states, at the very inception of their production or growth. . ."

Another decision of that court is that the manufacture of sugar within the state had under the facts there presented no direct relation to commerce between the states or with foreign nations, and that such manufacture was not subject to regulation by Congress, even though the products of the refineries were sold and distributed in several states. It appeared in that case that all the companies owning and operating the refineries were engaged in interstate trade or commerce, and the court seemed to be of the opinion that interstate commerce was indirectly affected.[6]

[5a] *Heisler* v. *Thomas Colliery Co.* 260 U. S. 245 (1922).
[6] *United States* v. *E. C. Knight Co.*, 156 U. S. 1 (1894).

In the famous Child Labor decision,[7] the Act of September 1, 1916, prohibiting the transportation in interstate commerce of goods made in a factory in which thirty days prior to their removal therefrom children under the age of 14 years had been employed or permitted to work, or children between the ages of 14 and 16 years had been employed or permitted to work more than eight hours in one day or more than six days in any one week, or after the hour of 7 P.M., or before the hour of 6 A.M., was held unconstitutional as transcending the commerce power of the Congress and invading the powers reserved to the states. Again the court reiterated the doctrine that the manufacture of goods is not commerce, nor do the facts that they are intended for and are afterwards shipped in interstate commerce make their production a part of that commerce subject to the control of the Congress.

By another decision[8] arising under the Sherman law, the United Mine Workers of America were acquitted of a charge of combining to interfere with interstate commerce on the ground that the mining of coal was not interstate commerce, even though the coal after reaching the surface was shipped to points in other states. Obstruction to coal mining is not a direct obstruction to interstate commerce in coal, although it may affect it by reducing the amount of coal to be carried in that commerce. To amount to a conspiracy under the Sherman Act an intention to restrain interstate commerce must be proved, or there must be so direct and substantial an effect upon interstate commerce that such intention may be reasonably inferred.

In these and other cases the point was definitely de-

[7] *Hammer* v. *Dagenhart,* 247 U. S. 251 (1917).

[8] *United Mine Workers of America* v. *Coronado Coal Co.,* 259 U. S. 344 (1921).

cided that production and manufacture are not in themselves interstate commerce and are exclusively within the regulation of the states. The Recovery Act directly regulates all manufacture and production. It plainly regulates production within a state of goods consumed within the same state.

It is also clear that the Supreme Court has not heretofore recognized an absolute power in Congress to exclude goods from interstate commerce. The constitutionality of the licensing power vested in the President under the Recovery Act could only be supported by the assumption of such an absolute power.

In the so-called Lottery case[9] the power of Congress to exclude lottery tickets from interstate commerce was upheld, the court justifying its decision on the unique ground that commerce was being "polluted" by the practice. By the Act of 1912 prize fight films and pictures were excluded from interstate and foreign commerce on moral grounds.[10] The Webb-Kenyon Act was upheld prohibiting the transportation of liquor from one state into another state in violation of the laws of the latter.[11] The Child Labor decision, to which reference has been made, is a very distinct and definite limitation on the power of Congress to exclude goods from interstate commerce.

Opponents of the law will argue that to recognize the existence of an absolute power of exclusion would be to ignore completely the most basic of constitutional conceptions, that is, the separation of powers between the federal and state governments. It will be conceded that the Supreme Court may validly determine that Congress has the power to exclude persons and property from

9 188 U. S. 321 (1903).
10 *United States* v. *Johnston,* 232 Fed. 970 (1916).
11 *Clark Distillery Co.* v. *Western Maryland R. R.,* 242 U. S. 311 (1917).

transportation in interstate commerce in order to prevent generally recognized evils, but a statute which deals with this power as an absolute power goes far beyond all sound constitutional principles. It will be vigorously argued that the complete scope of the commerce regulation in the Recovery Act and the autocratic powers which that Act gives the President to exclude companies from engaging in business in or affecting interstate commerce are void because beyond the power of Congress.

Proponents of constitutionality, on the other hand, find aid and comfort from another distinct line of decisions of the Supreme Court. Most of these are recent and their effect is to broaden the power of Congress over commerce to embrace all transactions *in* or *affecting* or even *influencing* interstate or foreign commerce. These decisions proceed upon the theory that transactions local in their situs and nature may so affect interstate commerce as to interrupt its flow or unduly interfere with or burden it and therefore the supreme power of Congress to protect, foster and control interstate commerce implies its power to deal with such transactions. This reasoning furnishes the basis, if there is a basis, for that exercise of power over all trade and commerce which is inherent in the Recovery Act.

The leading decision which directly upholds the exercise of the regulative power of Congress under the Commerce Clause, not only as extending to interstate commerce as such, but to all acts which affect interstate commerce and which sanctions the exercise of power over local business as a means of effectively regulating interstate business, is the so-called Shreveport case.[12] There the Interstate Commerce Commission found that a certain local tariff prescribed by the Texas Railroad

[12] *Houston & Texas Ry.* v. *United States,* 234 U. S. 342, 353 (1913).

Commission worked a discrimination against interstate commerce and ordered the carrier to charge a higher rate within the State of Texas than was authorized by the Texas Railroad Commission. The Supreme Court of the United States upheld this power and said that "Congress in the exercise of its paramount power may prevent the common instrumentalities of interstate and intrastate commercial intercourse from being used in their intrastate operations to the injury of interstate commerce." "That is not to say," declared the court, "that Congress possesses the authority to regulate the internal commerce of a state, as such, but that it does possess the power to foster and protect interstate commerce, and to take all measures necessary or appropriate to that end, although intrastate transactions of interstate carriers may thereby be controlled."

Since the Shreveport case, the Supreme Court has consistently held that the Congress may control strictly intrastate activities whenever they tend to burden or interfere with interstate commerce.[13]

The interference is sufficiently close to permit congressional regulation when the price fixed by the intrastate transactions influences the interstate prices for the same commodities;[14] or when intrastate rates yield a return below that authorized for interstate carriers.[15] The Interstate Commerce Commission was held justified in controlling the accounts of interstate carriers, even to the extent of requiring accounts of intrastate transactions, including those of a subsidiary whose business was to run an amusement park entirely located in one state.[16]

The Chicago Board of Trade case is illuminating.

13 *Stafford* v. *Wallace,* 258 U. S. 495 (1922).

14 *Board of Trade* v. *Olsen,* 262 U. S. 1 (1923).

15 *Railroad Comm. of Wisconsin* v. *C. B. & Q. Ry.,* 257 U. S. 563 (1922).

16 *Interstate Commerce Commission* v. *Goodrich Transit Co.,* 224 U. S. 194 (1912).

That case involved the constitutional validity of the Grain Futures Act of September 21, 1922. That statute placed Grain Boards of Trade under complete federal supervision and regulation. It regulated memberships on the Board and conditions of memberships and legislated with regard to the rules governing the conduct of its business. Chief Justice Taft delivered the opinion of the Supreme Court. He upheld the validity of the statute under the Commerce Clause on the theory that all of the activities of the Board of Trade directly or indirectly affected interstate commerce.

In 1921 Congress enacted a law for the control of packers and stockyards. Prior to the passage of that Act it had been assumed that trading in hogs and cattle after they had arrived at stockyards in Chicago, Kansas City, Omaha, and other points, was strictly local commerce. The purchases and sales were begun and completed in the live stock exchanges and were considered as local a transaction as the purchase of flour in a grocery. The constitutionality of the regulation of the business by the Congress was challenged and when it reached the Supreme Court the statute was upheld. The Court made this notable declaration as to the scope of the Commerce Clause:

"Obviously, that power, [the interstate commerce power] if it is to exist, must include the authority to deal with obstructions to interstate commerce, and with a host of other acts, which, because of their relation to and influence upon interstate commerce, come within the power of Congress to regulate, although they are not interstate commerce in and of themselves."[17]

The Sherman law provided for the punishment of persons combining to restrain commerce between the states. It has been held not necessary that

[17] *Stafford* v. *Wallace,* 258 U. S. 495 (1922).

the persons combining be actually engaged in interstate commerce to come within the prohibition of that law. The law has been applied to laboring groups who by concerted action have prevented goods from entering into interstate commerce.[18] Emphasis is laid by the courts on the natural effect of the acts complained of being such as to affect and restrict the normal flow of interstate commerce. Intent is not the major element, but the closeness of the connection between the action taken and interstate commerce constitutes the basis of the decision.

From this review of decisions of the Supreme Court it is apparent that the doctrine of the inherently flexible and adaptive nature of constitutional provisions applies with peculiar force to the Commerce Clause.

Will the Supreme Court now sanction a further enlarged application of that clause? Will it uphold the validity of the comprehensive provisions of the Recovery Act on the theory that the Congress declared, in enacting the statute, that a national emergency productive of widespread unemployment and disorganization of industry burdened interstate and foreign commerce and affected the public welfare, and that to meet such emergency and to remove all obstructions to the free flow of interstate and foreign commerce which tended to diminish the amount thereof, it was necessary to control all of the trade and business of the country? Will the Court sanction the legislative scheme of national unified control as a reasonable exercise of power, because without it under the existing crisis interstate commerce could not be effectively and completely protected, fostered, promoted and controlled?

[18] *Bedford Cut Stone Co.* v. *Journeymen Stone Cutters Assn. of North America*, 274 U. S. 37.

But the indubitable deduction from all the decisions of the Supreme Court is that the principle still prevails that the commerce which Congress regulates is interstate or foreign commerce, and that its power to control intrastate transactions extends only to such local transactions as in reality affect interstate and foreign commerce.

There must be a factual basis for the exercise of power. Transactions which do not actually enter into interstate commerce, or which do not in some real manner affect interstate commerce, are not subject to federal regulation. For the exercise of national power over local transactions, it must appear that such local transactions in some actual manner are interfering with the flow of interstate commerce or creating burdens upon interstate commerce. This is the doctrine today of the Supreme Court of the United States.

In its first decision, dealing with the constitutionality of the Future Trading Act, the Court declared:

> "They [business transactions] cannot come within the regulatory power of Congress as such, unless they are regarded by Congress, from the evidence before it, as directly interfering with interstate commerce, so as to be an obstruction or burden thereon." [19]

In every case in which the court has upheld the regulation of transactions local in their situs and nature, it has been careful to point out the direct relation between interstate commerce and the activity or object local in nature which Congress was regulating. A remote and incidental effect upon interstate trade is insufficient.[20] The relation and effect must be more than "accidental, secondary, remote or merely probable." [21]

[19] *Hill* v. *Wallace,* 259 U. S. 44 (1922).
[20] *Penn. Sugar Refining Co.* v. *American Sugar Refining Co.,* 166 Fed. 254 (1908).
[21] *Swift & Company* v. *United States,* 196 U. S. 375.

"Affect," as used in the statute, must be given a reasonable application; it must refer to local activities which obstruct, interfere with or place a burden on interstate commerce.

There are many transactions in trade and industry which are strictly and exclusively local and internal within a state and which in no real way relate to or affect interstate commerce. The assumption that all business in every hamlet in the country affects interstate commerce can be repelled by a hundred examples. Some of the most obvious and unquestionable are the services in restaurants, barber shops, hotels, custom tailors, shoemakers, and a large category of service occupations. As to such transactions there is no real constitutional basis for the exercise of federal power. If the Recovery Act is construed to embrace all trade and industry, then it extends to transactions which are strictly and exclusively and unquestionably local in their nature and effect, with no actual relation to interstate commerce. The conclusion seems inescapable that a federal statute applying to such transactions is too broad and transcends the power of Congress.

The NRA has been overambitious. The application of the Recovery Act and of codes to business has been too extreme and has been overdone. Effective and complete enforcement is not feasible. In a country so vast as this, with its 120,000,000 people and its infinite variety of conditions, the detailed regulation of all business through a central government bureau is a human impossibility. The repetition of this point may appear as the too emphatic urging of the obvious. We have already reached the conclusion that the formulation of codes must be restricted on grounds of expediency and wisdom and necessity. The same conclusion now seems justified upon grounds of law. Persistence in the exertion of the powers under the Recovery Act to regulate all business of every kind and nature will imperil the validity of the whole NRA.

Extremely difficult indeed will it be for the courts to construe the statute itself as not covering strictly and exclusively local transactions, but the Supreme Court may do so, and by such interpretation validate it, but confine its operation to transactions in and affecting interstate commerce, thus bringing it within the scope of the Commerce Clause.

The Act can be held to be too broad and its application to certain persons or circumstances invalid without completely annulling it, because it contains this carefully worded saving provision:

"Sec. 303. If any provision of this Act, or the application thereof to any person or circumstances, is held invalid, the remainder of the Act, and the application of such provision to other persons or circumstances, shall not be affected thereby."

The framers of the Act were not free from doubt as to its constitutionality if applied to all trade and commerce. Mr. David L. Podell, one of the framers of the statute, in speaking before the American Bar Association, used this language:

"Everybody who had anything to do with the framing of the Act realized that the question was inherent in the document. You couldn't frame any act that would deal with the national situation as it was presented without involving it in that question of Interstate Commerce and constitutionality." [22]

In dealing with the constitutional basis of power for the adoption of this statute, three courses are open:

[22] 20 *American Bar Ass'n. Jour.*, p. 283, May, 1934.

The Supreme Court may hold that under the conditions existing in June, 1933, all of the commercial and industrial activities of the nation directly or indirectly affected interstate and foreign commerce and therefore the inclusion of all trade and industry within the Act is not beyond the scope of the Commerce Clause.

That would be a decision that constitutional power extended to the whole Act.

It may be held that under the conditions existing in June, 1933, there was no basis, in fact, for the assumption that all the commercial and industrial activities of the nation directly or indirectly affected interstate and foreign trade, and therefore a statute embracing all trade and industry was broader than the Commerce Clause.

That would be a decision that the whole Act is a nullity for lack of constitutional power.

The provisions of the Recovery Act may be strained to the construction that the statute applies only to interstate and foreign commerce and to local activities and objects which have a direct relation to and effect upon interstate and foreign commerce, and that the statute is valid only so far as it regulates interstate and foreign commerce, all other commerce being excluded.

That would be a decision that there is constitutional basis for the Act in a restricted operation.

If the Recovery Act comes within the jurisdiction of the Supreme Court in a controversy involving the Constitution the questions suggested must there be answered. No answer except that of the Supreme Court is important.

CHAPTER IX

DUE PROCESS OF LAW

IF IT is concluded that the Commerce Clause is a sufficient basis of power for the enactment of the Recovery Act, either in complete or restricted operation, the question remains as to whether the power has been exerted in a manner consistent with the limitations of the Constitution. Legislative power may plainly exist, but its exercise by Congress may contravene one or more of the restraints of the Constitution. The constitutional validity of the Recovery Act must first be judged with reference to the basic power for its enactment. That matter I discussed in the preceding chapter. It must also be tested by the limitations in the Constitution on the exercise of federal power. By this test the Act is invalid if its provisions, when applied and in operation, deprive the citizen of liberty or property without due process of law.

The Federal Constitution (Amendment V) declares that no person "shall be deprived of life, liberty, or property without due process of law; nor shall private property be taken for public use without just compensation."

This command applies to action by the Federal Government and governs the Recovery Act and its administration. There is a similar restraint on the action of the several states embodied in the Fourteenth Amendment.

In this discussion we shall be primarily concerned with those individual rights connoted in the term "liberty" and with the restraints on liberty found within the Recovery Act and the codes promulgated under it.

Due process of law "is intended to secure the individual from the arbitrary exercise of the powers of government, unrestrained by the established principles of private rights and distributive justice."[1] Its essential meaning is that in America liberty shall never be destroyed by arbitrary power.

It is not liberty as a mere abstraction or as an ancient principle with which we are concerned, but as a living human right under concrete conditions. We deal with liberty in relation to human values and social welfare. Many restraints on liberty are justified and are entirely consistent with the principles of the Constitution. Restraints on individual liberty have been sanctioned where social welfare or public necessity plainly require such restraints. Every holder of property, however absolute his title, holds it under the implied condition that its use shall not be injurious to the community.[2] Extreme, arbitrary, unnecessary and unreasonable restraints on freedom and on the use of property have been held by the Supreme Court to be in violation of the Constitution.

In a recent decision of the Supreme Court this statement appears:

". . . The liberty of the individual to do as he pleases, even in innocent matters, is not absolute. It must frequently yield to the common good and the line beyond which the power of interference may not be pressed is neither definite nor unalterable but may be made to move within limits not well defined with changing need and circumstance. Any attempt to fix a rigid boundary would be unwise as well as futile. . ."[3]

The axiom that "circumstances give in reality to every principle its distinguishing color and distinguishing effect" applies with special force to the principle of due

[1] Black's *Constitutional Law* (1910), page 573.
[2] *Holden* v. *Hardy,* 169 U. S. 363.
[3] *Atkins* v. *Children's Hospital,* 261 U. S. 525, 561.

process of law. That principle protects the freedom of the individual from legislative and executive power, but the conception of individual freedom has changed under changing conditions and from generation to generation. Due process is not an absolute rule of law but a principle of justice to be applied under concrete conditions. It implies certain immutable principles of justice which inhere in the very idea of free government.[4] Judicial interpretation of due process as a protection of the freedom of the individual has been progressively changing under new social and economic conditions, but when that interpretation reaches the stage where any limitation on individual freedom by an act of the Congress or executive order is to be sanctioned judicially then this constitutional principle has wholly ceased to function.

The recurring problem of determining the reasonableness and necessity of restraints on liberty through legislative power is ever before the Supreme Court. "These correlative rights, that of the citizen to exercise exclusive dominion over property and freely to contract about his affairs, and that of the state to regulate the use of property and the conduct of business, are always in collision." [5] In dealing judicially with this grave problem under modern complex economic conditions there is, in the language of Mr. Chief Justice Hughes, "a growing appreciation of public needs and of the necessity of finding ground for a rational compromise between individual rights and public welfare."

In its recent decision in the Nebbia case the Supreme Court reaffirmed an ancient doctrine:

"Thus has this court from the early days affirmed that the power to promote the general welfare is inherent in govern-

[4] *Holden* v. *Hardy,* 169 U. S. 363.
[5] *People* v. *Nebbia,* 54 Sup. Ct. 510 (1934).

ment. Touching the matters committed to it by the Constitution, the United States possesses the power, as do the states in their sovereign capacity touching all subjects, jurisdiction of which is not surrendered to the Federal Government . . ."

But likewise that court has always emphatically affirmed the doctrine that the exercise of the power to promote the general welfare must not arbitrarily or unreasonably deprive the citizen of his liberty or property without due process of law.

All enactments under the Commerce Clause of the Constitution are limited by the application and force of the due process provision.[6] The Due Process Clause of the Constitution governs the provisions of the Recovery Act and all that has been done or is to be done under the statute and in its administration. Has the Congress exercised its power in a manner and to a degree violative of due process in taking the property or restricting the liberty of the citizen? Are the Act and the codes under it an unjust and arbitrary restriction on the rights of ownership?[7] Are the means and methods adopted and authorized proper and valid regulations, are they necessary and reasonable, or are they extreme, unreasonable, capricious, arbitrary, directly destroying or abridging freedom of action and liberty of contract and the use and ownership of property?

Three essential and important provisions of the statute must be tested under the due process clause. They are:

> The power granted to the President to impose involuntary or compulsory codes, fixing maximum hours of labor, minimum rates of pay, and other conditions of employment, in trade or industry.

[6] *Chicago, Rock Island, etc. Ry.* v. *United States* (1931), 284 U. S. 80. Compare *Adair* v. *United States,* 208 U. S. 161.

[7] 284 U. S. 97.

The mandatory provisions for collective bargaining.

Section 5 (b) giving the President power to require a license as a condition of engaging in business in or affecting interstate or foreign commerce.

Codes formulated under the statute and approved by the President become in legal effect a part of the statute. They have the same force as the statute. All provisions of codes must therefore be tested as to their validity by the basic principle that no man shall be deprived of liberty or property without due process of law.

Existing codes restrain the liberty of the citizen by a great variety of provisions. Typical provisions imposing mandatory requirements are the following:

No factory may be operated during any week for more than 40 hours.

For overtime work one and one-half wages must be paid.

All employees must be paid wages equal to or above a specified minimum.

All members of an industry must contribute to the expenses of the administration and enforcement of the code.

Equitable adjustment of wages must be made and in so doing no wages are to be reduced.

Employers in fixing wages and working conditions must deal in collective bargaining with such representatives as are selected by the workmen.

Every employer is prohibited from discharging a man because he is a member of a labor organization of his own choosing.

Employers may not fix as conditions of employment that their employees shall join any employee organization.

Restrictions on expansion of plant and production facilities.

Other restrictions of the liberty of the individual are:

No citizen dissenting from a code may bid for government work.

A citizen refusing to display the Code Blue Eagle will be boycotted under government influence and action.

These and numerous other restrictions on individual liberty are found in existing codes and regulations. They obviously destroy or curtail freedom of action in matters always considered of vital importance. They apply to all merchants and manufacturers, large and small. They apply to every character of business, with no regard to the oft repeated dogma that a business to be regulated by the government must be affected with a public interest. Is the power to limit hours of work, fix minimum wages and prescribe all working conditions, in every trade and industry in the country, actually required by public interest, or is it a power so vast and drastic as to be arbitrary and unreasonable?

The Due Process Clause, of course, has no relation to the free and voluntary coöperation, under codes, which exists now upon a vast scale. Such freedom of association and coöperation of merchants and manufacturers is not only consistent with constitutional liberty but is an expression of it. It is plain that those who voluntarily accept and assent to a code cannot invoke the doctrine that the operation of its provisions unduly deprives them of liberty or property. It is only where a code, or amendment to a code, has been imposed upon a trade or industry without its consent, or where an individual member of the industry dissents and rejects a code and it is forced upon him by virtue of the statute, that the constitutional principle can apply.

In discussing the grave question as to what restraints on liberty by legislative or executive action are necessary and justified, we enter a field of political and economic controversy. We treat of matters which go to the very heart of the New Deal. Many will argue that the curtailment of freedom of action found in the Recovery Act and in its administration is economically sound. Others will contend that the sounder economic policy is based on a wider measure of initiative and freedom in business enterprise. One school of thought will argue that restrictions on liberty through government action promote the social welfare. Another school will vigorously proclaim the human significance and the social and economic value of liberty.

Here also we deal with matters which go to the very foundation of our institutions, with rights which have been fondly proclaimed as indestructible and inalienable. A wide measure of individual freedom of thought and action is of the essence of our constitutional system. It is this which gives it the sharp contrast to Sovietism, Fascism and Naziism. With England and Czechoslovakia, two other outstanding examples, we adhere to a régime based on the principles of civil liberty. Other parts of the habitable world are also governed by liberal and democratic institutions. Happily we are not

> "This last spot of earth where Freedom now
> Stands single in her only sanctuary."[8]

A process of whittling down liberty and enlarging governmental power over the actions of citizens is hard to arrest or moderate. Power feeds upon power and grows into tyranny. The framers of the Constitution "foresaw that troublous times would arise, when rulers and people would become restive under restraint, and seek by sharp and decisive measures to accomplish ends deemed just and proper; and that the principles of constitutional liberty would be in peril, unless established by irrepealable law. The history of the world had taught them that what was done in the past might be attempted in the future."[9]

[8] Wordsworth, William, *The Prelude,* XI, 400.
[9] Ex Parte *Milligan,* 4 Wall. (U. S.), 2.

"Looking back over the history of mankind we see that it consists in the successive rise and decay of great civilizations. Are we also destined to plunge downward to stagnation or decay? Or may we, *by taking thought,* hope to escape the common fate of all our predecessors?"[10]

There is no inexorable law of decay in civilizations.[10a] No nemesis of blind forces predetermines the end of free institutions. The fault is not in our stars but in ourselves. "Principles have not failed," says President Thomas G. Masaryk of Czechoslovakia; "men have failed." It is not overstressing the gravity of the situation now to say we are facing a crisis in our constitutional system. Will its restraints and limitations continue with dynamic force, or will they become devitalized and mere form? How far will the power of government go and be sustained? What is the drift of the Supreme Court? What are the philosophic and legal concepts of that supreme arbiter of our social and economic destiny?

Here again we find the Court has declared principles and applied doctrines which apparently are an insurmountable barrier to the validity of the Recovery Act. The reasoning must be abandoned and these doctrines must be qualified under the impelling force of the economic emergency before that Court can give its sanction to the provisions of the statute and of codes.

Prior decisions of the Court in defense of individual liberty deal with many attempts of the legislative power to impose restraints which have been held arbitrary and unwarranted.

The broad conception of liberty often declared and

[10] Quoted from William McDougall in *Mankind at the Crossroads,* by Edward M. East, page 42. Scribner.

[10a] Read the brilliant essay entitled, "Decadence" in "Essays Speculative and Political," by the Rt. Hon. A. J. Balfour, published London, Hodder & Stoughton, Ltd. (1920).

applied by the Supreme Court was stated in a decision late in the past century in these words:

"The Liberty mentioned in that amendment [the Fourteenth Amendment] means not only the right of the citizen to be free from the mere physical restraint of his person, as by incarceration, but the term is deemed to embrace the right of the citizen to be free in the enjoyment of all his faculties; to be free to use them in all lawful ways; to live and work where he will; to earn his livelihood by any lawful calling; to pursue any livelihood or avocation and for that purpose to enter into all contracts which may be proper, necessary and essential to his carrying out to a successful conclusion the purposes above mentioned." [11]

Early in this century the New York legislature enacted a law that no employee should be permitted or required to work in a baking establishment more than sixty hours in any one week or more than ten hours in any one day. The Supreme Court of the United States held then that the statute interfered unreasonably and arbitrarily with the freedom of contract between employer and employee, and that it was not a proper exercise of the police power of the state, being neither in the interest of the public morals, public health, nor public safety. The court declared:

". . . The general right to make a contract in relation to his business is part of the liberty of the individual protected by the Fourteenth Amendment of the Federal Constitution. *Allgeyer* v. *Louisiana,* 165 U. S. 578. Under that provision no State can deprive any person of life, liberty or property without due process of law. . ." [12]

In a case holding invalid another state statute restraining a manufacturer in dealing with employees, the court used this language:

[11] *Allgeyer* v. *Lousiana,* 165 U. S. 578 (1897).
[12] *Lochner* v. *New York,* 198 U. S. 45 (1905).

". . . The Act, as the construction given to it by the state court shows, is intended to deprive employers of a part of their liberty of contract, to the corresponding advantage of the employed and the upbuilding of the labor organizations. But no attempt is made, or could reasonably be made, to sustain the purpose to strengthen these voluntary organizations, any more than other voluntary associations of persons, as a legitimate object for the exercise of the police power. They are not public institutions, charged by law with public or governmental duties, such as would render the maintenance of their membership a matter of direct concern to the general welfare. . .

". . . But the Fourteenth Amendment, in declaring that a State shall not 'deprive any person of life, liberty or property without due process of law,' gives to each of these an equal sanction; it recognizes 'liberty' and 'property' as co-existent human rights, and debars the States from any unwarranted interference with either."[13]

In dealing with the regulation of a private business by legislative measures the Supreme Court declared in another decision that "to justify the state in thus interposing its authority in behalf of the public it must appear, first, that the interests of the public generally as distinguished from those of a particular class require interference; and second, that the means are reasonably necessary for the accomplishment of the purpose, and not unduly oppressive upon individuals. The legislature may not under the guise of protecting the public interest arbitrarily interfere with private business or impose unusual and unnecessary restrictions upon lawful occupations. In other words, its determination as to what is a proper exercise of its police powers is not final or conclusive, but is subject to the supervision of the courts."[14]

[13] *Coppage* v. *Kansas,* 236 U. S. 1, 16 (1914). See also *Adair* v. *United States,* 208 U. S. 161, 174 (1907).
[14] *Lawton* v. *Steele,* 152 U. S. 133 (1894).

The court has often declared that freedom in the making of contracts of personal employment is an elementary part of the rights of personal liberty and private property, and cannot be arbitrarily interfered with consistently with due process of law.

Direct interference with production and with those processes by which wealth is distributed among the people is not, according to the Supreme Court, as evidenced by its past decisions, a valid function of government. The court has affirmed that so long as the institutions of private property and freedom of contract prevail, the inequalities of fortune are a necessary incident of commercial dealings and a normal result of our economic order. With regard to governmental regulation of prices as to ordinary occupations, the court has stated:

> "It has never been supposed since the adoption of the Constitution that the business of the butcher or the baker or the tailor, woodchopper, mining operator or the miner, was clothed with such a public interest that the prices of his product or his wages could be fixed by state regulation . . .;"

and accordingly it was held that the state could not regulate the price of theatre admissions, charges of an employment agency, or the retail sales price of gasoline.[15]

A unanimous court held that it was unconstitutional as a means of securing a continuous supply for the public of essential commodities and services, for the state to require employers and employees to settle their differences by a resort to a so-called court of industrial relations rather than by strike or lockout.[16]

It has also been held not to be within the power of government for the purpose of preventing overproduc-

[15] *Williams* v. *Standard Oil Co.*, 278 U. S. 235 (1929).
[16] *Wolff Packing Co.* v. *Court of Industrial Relations*, 262 U. S. 522 (1923).

tion and disastrous price-cutting, to require that one should secure a state license before engaging in the business of the artificial manufacture of ice. The court declared that "a regulation which has the effect of denying or unreasonably curtailing the common right to engage in a lawful private business . . . cannot be upheld consistently with the Fourteenth Amendment."[17]

Opinions of the highest court abound with strong and at times impassioned declarations of the sanctity of the rights of ownership and the liberty of contract; of the inviolate right of men freely to apply their energies and freely pursue their own lawful vocations and callings and businesses; of the human dignity and the economic and social value which inhere in the preservation of liberty; with affirmations that fundamental individual rights are indestructible so long as our constitutional system endures. For over a century a philosophy of virile individualism has permeated the decisions of the court, repelling successive arbitrary encroachments by government upon individual freedom of action.

As late as 1926 the court declared:

"If the state may compel the surrender of one constitutional right as a condition of its favor it may in like manner compel a surrender of all. It is inconceivable that guarantees imbedded in the Constitution of the United States may thus be manipulated out of existence."[18]

And in 1932 we find the court reaffirming:

"The principle is imbedded in our constitutional system that there are certain essentials of liberty with which the state is not entitled to dispense in the interest of experiments. . ."

[17] *New State Ice Co.* v. *Liebmann,* 285 U. S. 262 (1932).
[18] *Frost Trucking Co.* v. *Railroad Comm. of California,* 271 U. S. 577 (1926).

Personal and economic freedom are of the essence of our constitutional system. This, we believe, has been abundantly shown from successive decisions of the highest court.

But we are now to inquire what happens to these constitutional principles under the impact of a grave financial crisis or economic emergency. The answer is that individual freedom of action can then be restrained if not destroyed by extraordinary economic measures in the interest of general security and welfare. This is the theme of recent pronouncements from the Supreme Court. Based on the existence of an emergency, the Court has held valid a law which authorized by judicial action the extension of the time for the redemption from existing mortgages,[19] and has upheld the validity of the New York statute authorizing the fixing of a minimum price in the sale of milk.[20] The Adamson Law, fixing railroad wages for from 7 to 11 months in order to avoid a serious railroad strike, was held constitutional, in spite of the fact that it clearly involved an interference with freedom of contract.[21] Likewise, during the post-war period, the housing shortage was held to justify the fixing of rents by government action for the period of emergency.[22] The legislative action in these cases was declared to be of an emergency nature and limited in time.

In the year 1923 the Supreme Court, speaking of its own decision six years before which upheld the Adamson Law, said that that decision "went to the border line although it concerned an interstate common

19 *Home Building & Loan Assn.* v. *Blaisdell,* supra.
20 *People* v. *Nebbia* (supra).
21 *Wilson* v. *New,* 243 U. S. 332 (1917).
22 *Block* v. *Hirsch,* 256 U. S. 135 (1921).

carrier in the presence of a nation-wide emergency and the possibility of a great disaster." [23]

The Supreme Court in considering the Recovery Act will be moved by the conditions of a grave emergency. It will deal with a law which in its opening sentence declares the existence of a national emergency productive of widespread unemployment and disorganization of industry, which burdens interstate and foreign commerce, affects the public welfare and undermines the standards of living of the American people. So far as the Recovery Act restrains individual freedom of action, the court will consider its justness and reasonableness and necessity in the light of the background of the conditions under which it was enacted, the objectives it sought to achieve, the manner in which in its practical application it affects individual rights and the general welfare.

The economic policy and measures authorized by the broad regulations of the Recovery Act, declared by Congress necessary to meet the emergency and rehabilitate industry, may be upheld as proper regulations of interstate and foreign commerce by the same reasoning as was used by the court in sustaining the New York statute authorizing minimum prices for milk. Mr. Justice Roberts, who delivered the opinion of the court in that case, stated:

"So far as the requirement of due process is concerned, and in the absence of other constitutional restrictions, a state is free to adopt whatever economic policy may reasonably be deemed to promote public welfare, and to enforce that policy by legislation adapted to its purpose. . . Price control, like any other form of regulation, is unconstitutional if arbitrary, discriminatory, or demonstrably irrele-

[23] *Wolff Packing Co.* v. *Court of Industrial Relations,* 262 U. S. 522, 544 (1923).

vant to the policy which the legislature is free to adopt, and hence an unnecessary and unwarranted interference with individual liberty." [24]

Are all the restrictions on liberty of contract, on freedom of action in private business, necessarily involved in the application of the Recovery Act, in the statute and codes, a "rational compromise between individual rights and public welfare?" [25]

This is a problem of statesmanship and its solution rests with the Supreme Court. Statesmen of the front rank, as Beveridge spoke of Marshall, must make the fateful decision. It may be that by processes of argument similar to those by which the court recently sustained the statute of Minnesota impairing private contract rights, it may sanction the detailed regulations of all trade and industry by NRA through its codes which destroy individual freedom. It may decree that under the impelling emergency paramount public necessity required a total abandonment of the principle of "a business affected by a public interest," and required a single unified regulation and control national in scope and embracing every commercial and industrial activity; and that the mandatory provisions for codes and the compulsory executive and administrative powers were necessary to make such control real and effective. If and when that decision is rendered constitutional principles enshrined in prior decisions will, temporarily at least, cease to have restraining force. An economic crisis has made necessary—to quote the expressive phrase of an old English judge—the "inundation of the prerogative."

[24] *People* v. *Nebbia*, supra, page 516.
[25] Chief Justice Hughes in *Home Building & Loan Ass'n* v. *Blaisdell*, supra.

CHAPTER X

THE PRINCIPLE OF THE SEPARATION OF POWERS

IN THE vast sweep of events since the fourth of March, 1933, there are plainly evident two processes of change that may radically alter the structure of the government. Men may differ as to the wisdom of these changes or their influence on the future of the country, but no one can deny we live in a period of political transition and re-adjustment. Relocations of power are taking place in two directions. One is the enlargement of federal power and the dwarfing of the power of the states. It is shown by the concentration in the Federal Government of practically all power to legislate for the welfare of the people. The other redistribution of power is within the organization of the Federal Government. There we witness an extraordinary expansion of executive power and the subservience of the Congress. This shift of responsibility is an outstanding feature of the multiform legislation embraced within the New Deal.

Many acts of Congress have been attacked upon the ground that they have delegated legislative power to the executive branch of the government, but in the one hundred and forty-eight years of our history no one of them has ever been held void for that reason. Nevertheless, the principle of the separation of powers is imbedded in the structure of the government. It is one of the most important principles in our constitutional system. Washington in his Farewell Address warned the country against the consolidation of all the powers of government in one department. Madison wrote in the *Federalist* (No. 47):

"The accumulation of all powers, legislative, executive and judicial, in the same hands, whether of one, a few or many, whether hereditary, or self-appointed or elective, may justly be pronounced the very definition of tyranny."

John Adams wrote (*Works,* I, 186):

"It is by balancing one of these three powers against the other two that the efforts in human nature toward tyranny can alone be checked and restrained and any degree of freedom preserved."

Webster stated the same doctrine:

"The separation of the departments so far as practicable, and the preservation of clear lines between them is the fundamental idea in the creation of all of our constitutions and doubtless the continuance of regulated liberty depends on maintaining these boundaries." [1]

The division and distribution of powers are established in the Constitution.

Section 1 of Article I provides that "all legislative powers herein granted shall be vested in a Congress of the United States."

Section 1 of Article II reads: "The executive power shall be vested in a President of the United States of America."

Section 1 of Article III reads: "The judicial power of the United States shall be vested in one Supreme Court and in such inferior courts as the Congress may, from time to time, ordain and establish."

The Supreme Court has frequently stated that this doctrine of separation of powers is implicit in the Constitution.[2]

[1] For these quotations see Bondy, *The Separation of Governmental Powers,* Columbia University Studies.

[2] See *Field* v. *Clark,* 143 U. S. 649, 692 (1892); *Union Bridge Co.* v. *United States,* 204 U. S. 364, 381 (1907); *J. W. Hampton Co.* v. *United States,* 276 U. S. 394, 405 (1928).

The Recovery Act confers in broad terms practically uncontrolled discretionary power upon the President.

Section 10 (a) gives the President plenary power to prescribe such rules and regulations as he may deem necessary "to carry out the purposes of this Title," and the violation of any such rule or regulation is punishable by fine or imprisonment for not to exceed six months, or both.

Power is granted the President to impose involuntary or compulsory codes, fixing maximum hours of labor, minimum rates of pay, and other conditions of employment, in trade or industry.

Section 5 (b) gives the President the power to require a license as a condition of engaging in business in or affecting interstate or foreign commerce.

Under other sections the power of the President is equally unrestrained. His discretion is absolute and unlimited in fixing maximum hours of labor, minimum rates of pay, and other conditions of employment in the trade or industry or subdivision thereof. The only limitation is that his decrees must be such that they are reasonably appropriate to carry out the purposes of the Act, to rehabilitate industry, to relieve unemployment, eliminate unfair trade practices, to induce and maintain united action of labor and management and otherwise to provide for the general welfare.

The President may under such circumstances as he deems sufficient to justify the action, change or cancel customs duties, or limit or forbid imports, and the statute reads:

> "The decision of the President as to facts shall be conclusive."

The character and scope and gravity of the powers thus vested in the President need no comment. It has been argued that they are in effect a delegation of power to determine legislative policy, and to make laws, and not to execute laws or to enforce a policy laid down by Congress.

Are these delegations of power too broad to be constitutional?

The controlling principle of the separation of powers is that "a department may constitutionally exercise any power, whatever its essential nature, which has by the Constitution been delegated to it, but that it may not exercise powers not so constitutionally granted which, from their essential nature, do not fall within its division of government functions, unless such powers are properly incidental to the performance by it of its own appropriate functions."[3]

It has often been observed that the lines between the three great branches of the government cannot be drawn with exactness and that each of the three departments normally exercises powers which are not strictly within its province. For that reason the practical value and importance of the principle has been questioned, but all agree that in a case where powers essentially and plainly legislative in character are abdicated in favor of the executive branch of the government there is without question a violation of the Constitution. Only a plain and distinct and complete abdication of power from one branch to another violates the organic principle of separation of powers. The delegated power must be "strictly legislative" or "legislative in the highest sense" to be inseparable from the legislative department. Congress

[3] Willoughby on *The Constitution of the United States*, Vol. III, 2d Ed. pages 1616 ff.

has the exclusive power to determine primary or fundamental rules for the governing of future conduct. This power may not be devolved upon any other agency, but having exercised this power by promulgating the primary policy, Congress may confer upon some executive or administrative officer or body the authority to establish policies subordinate to and consistent with the legislative enactment.

This summary probably states the sound principle:

"We believe that our analysis of recent decisions by the Supreme Court of the United States sufficiently demonstrates that so long as it appears that the law-making body has gone as far as it reasonably can in the way of positive legislation and has only left to the administrative officers the filling in of details, that court will not declare a statute unconstitutional or void merely because no definite 'primary standard' has been established, and even though the function which the administrative officers perform may be legislative in its character." [4]

Although there is a wealth of dicta and text-book doctrine that legislative powers cannot be delegated, transfers of vast powers to the executive for the more efficacious execution of the laws have been constantly made by Congress and consistently upheld. A few of the decisions may be summarized. The power of the President to lower rates under the reciprocity provision of the McKinley Tariff Act was upheld.[5] A statute giving the Secretary of War power to order the removal of low or defective bridges did not involve an improper delegation.[6] The Interstate Commerce Commission was authorized by statute to designate standard height and

[4] *Illinois Law Review,* Vol. VII, 397, page 412.
[5] *Field* v. *Clark,* supra, 143 U. S. 649.
[6] *Union Bridge Co.* v. *United States,* supra.

maximum variations of drawbars for freight cars. The statute was held to be constitutional.[7] A statute giving the President power to change rates under a flexible tariff provision was likewise upheld.[8]

Notwithstanding its unbroken line of negative decisions dealing with this principle, the Supreme Court recently stated:

> "The functions of Government under our system are apportioned. To the Legislative Department has been committed the duty of making laws; to the Executive the duty of executing them; and to the Judiciary the duty of interpreting and applying them in cases properly brought before the courts. The general rule is that neither department may invade the province of the other, and neither may control, direct or restrain the action of the other. . ."[9]

Under the Recovery Act the question is a grave one: Has Congress here delegated to the President what is distinctly and concretely legislative power, in violation of that principle of separation of powers which is of the very essence of the structure of the Federal Government?

Congress in this statute has announced the legislative purpose in the most general terms. Reference to general welfare and to broad objectives of the statute are the only standards set up by the law for the making of rules and regulations for the control of industry. Practically unlimited discretion is vested in the President to make rules and regulations defining offenses punishable by fine and imprisonment. Exercising the powers conferred upon him by the Recovery Act, the President has issued an executive order which in effect assesses members of trade or industry for expenses of the administration and

[7] *St. Louis & Iron Mt. R. R.* v. *Taylor,* 210 U. S. 281 (1908).
[8] *J. W. Hampton, Jr. & Co.* v. *United States,* supra.
[9] *Massachusetts* v. *Mellon,* 262 U. S. 447.

enforcement of codes. Is this an exercise of the taxing power? The Constitution vests the taxing power in Congress. The President is vested with power to cancel, suspend or modify tariff duties, and the statute expressly declares that his decisions shall be conclusive as to the facts. Maximum hours and minimum wages and all other working conditions in industry may be prescribed in regulations and decrees embodied in executive orders. There can be no question but that the President is authorized by the Recovery Act to do things which are essentially legislative in nature.

A judge of a federal court of original jurisdiction has thus commented on the statute:

"... If the Congress may constitutionally delegate power as it has delegated it in the National Industrial Recovery Act, it is difficult to see why the Congress may not in an act declare that its policy is to provide for the general welfare of all the people, and that accordingly the President may promulgate such rules and regulations having the effect of law as will in his discretion best provide for the general welfare of all the people, and when that happens constitutionally, constitutional government as we have known it will cease to exist."

After that courageous statement, the learned judge quite indecisively continued:

"But while the principle that legislative power may not by Congress be delegated to other agencies of government, has been frequently announced, yet decisions which have held acts of Congress invalid because of violation of the principle are difficult or impossible to find. Accordingly this court, being one of the inferior courts contemplated by the Constitution, does not feel justified in declaring the act in question invalid because of the violation of the principle of constitutional law prohibiting the delegation of legislative power." [10]

[10] *United States* v. *Suburban Motor Service Corp.*, 5 Fed. Supp. 798 (1934).

Again the attitude and reasoning of the Supreme Court with respect to this phase of the Recovery Act will no doubt be conditioned by the emergency. In determining the validity of the broad and drastic powers transferred to the President that court will be moved by its own imaginative insight into the grave conditions that confronted the country in the month of June, 1933. Its final reasoning and conclusion may be that under the conditions then confronting the country there was an imperative need for immediate administrative and executive action of the character authorized by the statute; that the vesting of wide and discretionary powers of action was therefore a necessary and rational decision for the Congress to make if legislation was directly and effectively to deal with actual conditions. The vesting of truly legislative power in the President may be upheld because the formation of codes of fair competition for numberless diverse trades and industries necessarily requires broad discretionary power of decision and action, and an enumeration in the statute of its objectives was futile without transferring such powers to the Executive. This problem also must await the final word of the Supreme Court.

Departing from the question of law and viewing the policy of adherence to the principle of the separation of powers, it truly can be asserted that never in our history were the wisdom and necessity of that policy plainer than they are today.

Times of crisis undoubtedly require enlarged executive power and functions. Action to meet a crisis effectively and comprehensively must be concentrated in a single person acting under responsibility to the people. "Leadership and control," declared President Wilson, and this applies particularly to a crisis, "must be lodged somewhere; the whole art of statesmanship is the art of bringing the several parts of government into effective coöperation for the accomplishment of particular common objects—and party objects at that."

In a crisis extraordinary powers must be concentrated in the President and to him the country must look for moral and intellectual leadership. Executive leadership through great character was never more necessary. "One of the problems of democracy," wrote President Thomas G. Masaryk, "is how to put true and noble human quality into politics and the administration of the state."[11] Under the critical conditions now existing in this country and in the world it is equally imperative that we have two other strong and independent branches of government.

The New Deal has made even more preëminent the need of a great Supreme Court. The country will continue to require a court of profound learning, strength, wisdom, vision, invincible independence and unflinching courage. A staggering responsibility rests upon that court in passing upon the validity and adjudging the proper interpretation of the astonishing volume of new legislation.

Of supreme importance also is a strong and independent Congress. Congress has the primary responsibility for determining the solution of the problems which overshadow the nation. What form of regulations of industry will succeed the Recovery Act? What economic policy will be adopted? What new organs of government will be created to administer a regulative policy? How will the powers of taxation, borrowing and spending by the Federal Government be exercised? These are problems for Congress.

A strong legislative assembly for the nation is, in our

[11] *The Making of a State,* by Thomas Garrigue Masaryk, p. 460. Frederick A. Stokes & Co.

system of government, cardinal and fundamental. It should in spirit and quality reflect this vision of a great English statesman:

"I may speak of the House of Commons as a school of discipline for those who enter it. In my opinion it is a school of extraordinary power and efficacy. It is a great and noble school for the creation of all the qualities of force, suppleness and versatility of intellect. And it is also a great moral school. It is a school of temper. It is also a school of patience. It is a school of honor, and it is a school of justice."[12]

The composition of a strong Congress includes many elements. It should represent all interests, all the major divisions of human activity, and all points of view. It needs men of actual and wide experience in business; men who know by intimate contact and daily experience the infinitely diverse human problems involved in industry; who know by experience how legislative regulations actually work and should be applied; who know what is practical and what is impractical; who know what in concrete operation will promote economic welfare and what will do more harm than good. The cleavage between government and industry is fast disappearing. Future legislation will directly and vitally affect all economic activities. All signs of the times read that the NRA is only the first stage in some form of federal rulership of business. More and more the country will need sound ripened business judgment at the point where policies are determined and legislation formed to regulate industry.

Another necessary element in a strong representative Congress is a group of labor leaders or men deeply interested in the cause of labor. The millions of workers

[12] *Life of Gladstone,* by John Morley, Vol. 1, p. 86. Macmillan.

of the country should be represented in the Congress by men who by experience, sympathy, insight and character are qualified to speak for the cause of labor. The vital cause of these many millions of workers is not only in terms and conditions of work but also in education, independence, manhood and self-respect. Labor leadership with its vast power and influence has a deep responsibility in the devising of legislation for the economic well-being of the whole country.

A strong and independent Congress must include in its membership scholars in economics and political science. The distinction between political and economic problems has vanished. The exercise of all government power is conditioned upon a close study of social and economic facts. The contribution of universities to public life was never more essential and never before could be so beneficial. There is a lesson in the experience of England. Gladstone said:

> "There is not a feature or a point in the national character which has made England great among the nations of the world, that is not strongly developed and plainly traceable in our universities. For eight hundred or a thousand years they have been intimately associated with everything that has concerned the highest interest of the country." [13]

The need of great scholars in the legislative councils is conspicuously true under a system which does not permit experts from other departments to speak on the floor.

A powerful Congress unquestionably needs great lawyers ever conscious of the application of constitutional principles to government action. It is no exaggeration to say that the continued preservation of our constitutional system requires that in times of strain and stress we have men in Congress who have a genuine faith in

[13] *Ibid.*

free institutions and the power to fire such faith in others. "An emergency seems to arise," Senator Borah recently declared in the Senate, "and . . . we seem to doubt the methods and means provided by the founders of democracy. . . We have an emergency, and we employ instrumentalities to discredit our faith in democratic institutions. We need ancient faith, the ancient vision. . . Of these things this republic was built, and of these things alone it will be maintained. . . In the midst of the world turmoil Washington pinned his faith to constitutional democracy. . . In the midst of the fiercest hour of civil war Lincoln declared that government of the people, for the people, and by the people should not perish from the earth."

For a legislative department to diminish in power and sense of responsibility and independence is a grave misfortune. I quote a recent criticism of the work of the Congress by an able writer:

> "Rather the result is that legislation is 'more clearly determined by the preponderance of forces brought to bear upon legislative bodies than reasoned activity of the members.' Seldom are issues settled on the basis of social desirability; more often on 'expediency' and 'compromise.' The ends of the sessions are marked by a rushing and crowding of work; 'undue haste is essential if the measures are to get through before adjournment.' The whole arrangement is so desultory and disheartening that it is held in disrespect by many. It is so much so in fact that one observer has said, 'that the breakdown of legislative efficiency is one of the marked political phenomena of our time.'"[14]

Legislative problems and tasks are becoming increasingly vital. The most important powers of government are taxation and the spending of the public revenues.

[14] Albert J. Harno, in *American Bar Association Journal,* April 1933, p. 205.

These are within the exclusive control of Congress. The power of Congress to tax is practically unlimited. The absence of any restriction upon the taxing power is one of the most striking features of our constitutional system. Subject to the technical exceptions that Congress cannot tax instrumentalities of the states or exports and that it must impose direct taxes by the rule of apportionment, and indirect taxes by the rule of uniformity, the power to tax is unrestrained. It reaches every subject and may be exercised at discretion. The constitutional power to levy a tax on income means the power to take all incomes. The power to levy an excise tax on the transfer of an estate from a decedent to his heirs means the power to take the whole estate. Congress is not restrained by the Constitution. Its only restraint is its own wisdom, its sense of moral right, its judgment as to the soundness of economic policies. In a decision in 1904 the Supreme Court definitely abandoned any right to review an exercise of the power of taxation by Congress on the ground of improper motive or purpose.[15] In a very recent case the court again declared that the collateral purposes and motives of a legislation in levying a tax of any kind within the reach of its lawful power are matters beyond the scope of judicial inquiry.[16]

The power of Congress to spend is also unlimited. President Monroe vetoed an act appropriating federal funds to build the Cumberland Road in Pennsylvania on the ground that the construction of such internal projects was beyond the power of the Federal Government. In support of that veto he wrote a vigorous message. This

[15] *McCray* v. *United States,* 195 U. S. 27 (1904).

[16] The United States Supreme Court in *A. Magnano Co.* v. *Hamilton,* 54 Sup. Ct. 599 (1934).

Monroe doctrine as to federal appropriations did not have the vitality of his more famous one. The Supreme Court has since established that the power of Congress to appropriate public revenues is not limited by the Constitution. A taxpayer as such has no standing in court to question the constitutionality of an appropriation by Congress.[17] By Title II of the Recovery Act Congress by one stroke appropriated 3 and 3/10 billions. In its magnitude that action has few parallels in the history of any country. From published summaries it appears that Congress in fifteen months authorized the disbursement by the Federal Government of approximately $17,000,000,000, consisting of actual appropriations from the treasury of $12,000,000,000 and provisions for additional funds from the RFC to bring the sum to the grand total suggested.

The power of Congress to borrow has likewise no constitutional limitation. The power under the Constitution is thus succinctly phrased: "To borrow money on the credit of the United States." The exercise of that power resides in the discretion of Congress. The federal debt today is greater than in 1919 at the close of the War, greater than ever before in our history. It has reached astronomical figures beyond ordinary human comprehension. Roughly it is $27,000,000,000. The constitutionally unlimited taxing, borrowing and spending power of the Federal Government is the life-blood of the New Deal.

The power of taxation is exerted by the Congress consciously to destroy corporate organizations considered undesirable and as a medium for the redistribution of wealth. To confirm this statement, we need go back

[17] *Massachusetts* v. *Mellon,* 262 U. S. 447 (1922).

no further than the debates in the Senate with regard to the Revenue Act of 1934.[17a] The power of taxation is becoming the potent instrument of social and economic control. The future use of that power so vast and absolute will depend on the knowledge and wisdom of the Congress. For its abuse the only remedy of the people is political.[18]

The economic emergency created the necessity for an unprecedented enlargement of executive power. The same emergency has not lessened but has magnified the need of a strong and independent and wise Congress. Never before has the policy underlying the principle of the separation of powers, the necessity of three great co-ordinate but independent branches of the government, been more manifest or more vital.

17a See Congressional Record, vol. 78, p. 6129 (April 4, 1934), pp. 6135, 6240, 6243, 6668 (April 12, 1934).

18 "But if what Congress does," says the Supreme Court, "is within the limits of its power and is simply unwise or injurious, the remedy is that suggested by Chief Justice Marshall in *Gibbons* v. *Ogden,* when he said: 'The wisdom and the discretion of Congress, their identity with the people, and the influence which their constituents possess at elections, are, in this, as in many other instances, as that, for example, of declaring war, the sole restraints on which they have relied, to secure them from its abuse. They are the restraints on which the people must often rely solely, in all representative governments.'"

CHAPTER XI

CONCLUSION

"THE PEOPLE never give up their liberties," said Edmund Burke, "but under some delusion."[1] The world is on a holiday from first principles. The emphasis is on power and control and not freedom. In this country the rapid drift is to more and more government. The danger now is that the encroachments on individual rights and freedom will go farther than any real reasons of public welfare or social justice demand. The tendency to enlarge the power of government over men, once started, can hardly ever be brought to a close. The people looking to the government for favors and fortune not only tolerate but encourage the growth of power to the point of tyranny. Liberty is given up under the delusion that the essentials of the well-being of humankind can be created by the action of government.

The regulation of business implies business to regulate. The manifold processes of production must go on in private hands and under private initiative if that abundance is to be produced which is the foundation of general welfare. In a régime of freedom there is a free and spontaneous and productive play of the energies and highest faculties of men and women. "Coercion stifles power, and engenders all selfish desires and all the mean artifices of weakness. Coercion may prevent many transgressions; but it robs even actions which are legal of a portion of their beauty. Freedom may lead to many transgressions, but it lends even to vices a less ignoble form."[2] The functions and powers of free institutions

[1] Speech at the County Meeting of Bucks.
[2] Quoted from an Essay of Wilhelm Von Humboldt.

should be exerted to stimulate and inspire individual energy, ambition, initiative, inventiveness, organizing capacity, and freedom of association and coöperation, which lead to the general and vast production of wealth.

Production under economic freedom will adjust itself to human needs and desires. In a system in which there is freedom of choice by consumers the wants and demands of the people are potentially unlimited. With the exception of a few basic industries dealing in natural resources such as coal, oil and lumber, there is no overproduction of the goods needed by 120,000,000 people. One of the cardinal objectives of the Recovery Act is "to promote the fullest possible utilization of the present productive capacities of industries." To realize this objective capital must be induced to reënter productive enterprise. Corporations must be encouraged to expand their facilities so that they can employ labor for normal hours at fair wages. Individuals must have every incentive to organize new industries exploiting products of human invention. Time will always be developing new human needs and new products to meet such needs. The stupendous task of rehousing many millions of families will require an immeasurable use of manufactured products. Only upon an industrial system characterized by an irrepressible expansiveness of economic activities producing everything necessary to sustain and embellish life can there be built an orderly and happy nation.

Essential to a régime of freedom is the liberty of speech and publication. Spiritual freedom is closely related to constitutional and economic freedom. Stifle expression and you stifle invention and energy and growth. "Give the mind sea room." In many important countries contrary and critical opinion with respect to policies of goverment is suppressed by force. In this country between the people and the government free speech is an indestructible covenant.

> "And I announce as a glory of these States, that they respectfully listen to propositions, reforms, fresh views and doctrines, from successions of men and women.
> "Each age with its own growth!"[3]

A social and economic system built upon liberty and individualism produces excesses, injustices, tensions and maladjustments. Many of the evil conditions result from the corrupt designs and actions of men; others are the result of factors or a combination of circumstances which no individual can control. In recent years we have witnessed widespread privation in the midst of plenty, vast unemployment, waste and devastation of natural resources, unbalanced distribution and diminishing purchasing power, racketeering and banditry, flagrant breaches of trust by men in high places, gross disrespect for law, enormous and reckless growth of governmental and corporate debt, increasing concentration of wealth, deliberate destruction of goods essential to the wealth of the nation, ruinous competition, and widespread deterioration and destruction of capital. These conditions have created a social and economic order in which free industry cannot be justly and successfully conducted. Measures to abate or mitigate such evils and afflictions are within the function and responsibility of government. All its technique and power should be exerted to create an economic order of higher moral and legal standards.

As a direct consequence of the conditions that have developed in recent years from the abuses of liberty and extreme individualism we are in an era of greater government intervention and control. The emphasis is on the

[3] Walt Whitman.

social responsibility of business. This is the very essence of the New Deal, with all its tremendous innovations. It is an effort of government to exercise its highest functions. Every sign indicates that this movement will go forward and not backward. New plans and methods for social betterment and for the regulation of commerce and industry will be devised. A primary responsibility of those entrusted with power is to adjust and execute such plans consistently with the principles of civil liberty on which the government is founded.

The NRA was created to end or mitigate many evil conditions in industry developing in a period of *laissez-faire*. It will die but the good it has done should not be interred with its bones. Its record will be one of great achievements and great mistakes. The evils it has striven to combat and conquer will survive the statute which created it. What is to succeed the NRA? What new agency of the government will be erected for the national regulation of trade and industry? This is the most critical problem before the people of the country. During the coming year it will be a task for statesmanship of the highest order. Its solution will emerge from a conflict of opinions and convictions. Party politics has no place in the consideration or decision of this problem. The NRA has given the government an experience from which it should be able to determine what form of regulation and control is sound and what form is productive of harm. The intelligence of the nation has been enriched by the administration of the Recovery Act. "Men are only enlightened by feeling their way through experience."

Out of the experience of the NRA something constructive will come. It may be a permanent Industrial Control Statute. Such a statute, effective after June 16, 1935, seems almost certain of enactment. From the teachings of recent events deductions can be made as to some essential features of a new plan of regulation. The objectives of the new statute could be the same as those stated in Section 1 of the Recovery Act, but its provisions should be radically different. All arbitrary power should be eliminated. It should have no semblance of executive dictatorship. The power of the President to make rules and regulations subject to punishment by fine and imprisonment should have no place in the new statute; nor should there be absolute administrative power to impose involuntary or compulsory codes. Likewise the power to exact a license as a condition of participation in interstate commerce should rest in oblivion. The statute should be drawn with painstaking care to define plainly the character and measure of control of trade and industry which it proposes. The intent of the law should be to protect and safeguard the fullest measure of individual freedom consistent with public welfare and social justice.

Regulation of trades and industries under codes should be retained, but the procedure for codes should be primarily permissive and voluntary. The essence of the new scheme should be coöperative self-regulation through codes under the sanction and supervision of the government. Its primary purpose should be confined to the major economic activities of the nation but all trades and industries desiring to do so should have the privilege to make application for a code, and, through negotiations with the government, a code fitting the needs and conditions of the particular industry should be formed and approved. If a very large portion of the industry accepted or agreed to a code it should be binding on all members of the industry. Standardization and uniformity should be almost entirely avoided. Blanket codes, solely an emergency device, should have no place in the new economic policy. Industries should be dealt with on the basis of their own actual conditions, and the provisions of a code should be addressed to existing evils and undesirable conditions in the industry, and authorize the character and measure of association and coöperation which the conditions in the particular industry demand. Basic industries such as coal, oil and lumber should have especial consideration in framing the statute and in the formation of the codes.

Under exceptional circumstances involuntary or compulsory codes should be authorized. Such a code should be imposed upon a trade or industry only after a hearing and after a finding that there are prevalent in the industry conditions and evils which require government control under a compulsory code for the welfare of the industry, or its workers, or the protection of the public. The decision based upon such finding should specify the required provisions of the code, and when once promulgated it should be binding on the whole trade or industry. The finding and decision that such a code is necessary should be subject to judicial review.

The administration of such a statute will require a new commission. It should be composed of members appointed by the President, subject to confirmation by the Senate. One of them should be the Chairman or Director General. Vested in this commission will be the duty and responsibility of the just and impartial enforcement of the law. Rare judgment and wisdom and courage will be essential to the performance of that task.

The present organization of the NRA should be retained so far as deemed necessary in the administration of the new act. There should be regional organizations to decentralize administration and to maintain close contact with conditions throughout the country. The many great advances made by the NRA should be preserved. By its mistakes the new régime of regulation should profit.

Economic research and planning will be a division of the work of the new commission. A unit organized to that end should function as an advisory agency for government and industry, exercising only such powers as are compatible with constitutional and economic freedom. Experience will in all probability develop so that within such limitations the agency will have a wide sphere of usefulness. It will gather complete statistical information and furnish the means of measuring current economic social happenings as a basis for regulation. It will constantly study the application of codes and their effect on industry. It will make recommendations for the modification of codes and amendments of the statute based on knowledge derived from experience.

The National Labor Board or some similar labor commission should be continued as an auxiliary tribunal in the application and enforcement of the statute. No substitute has been suggested for such a national board with powers of mediation, conciliation and arbitration. It should actively function in developing principles upon which the united action of labor and management can be achieved. The reconciliation of great labor disputes, which menace the industrial peace of the nation and seem inevitable in the capitalistic system, will remain one of the supreme tasks of the government. Our industrial experience in the past half century shows that only the power of the national government can control the contending forces in a great strike.

The archaic and universally unsatisfactory anti-trust

laws should be repealed. Business cannot function except in an atmosphere of clarity of law. The new statute should specify by language free from doubt or ambiguity the practices and combinations which tend to create monopolies and which injure the people and are therefore condemned. The existence of these practices in an industry would be a circumstance to justify the imposition of a compulsory code of control and regulation. The functions of the Federal Trade Commission could be consolidated with the powers of the commission created by the new statute.

The administration and enforcement of codes should, as at present, be entrusted in the first instance to an organization within the industry. The government should continue to act and coöperate in the interpretation and application of codes. Strict and uniform and impartial enforcement of any existing code must be an essential plank in any new scheme and the commission must be equipped with all the powers and agencies necessary to maintain such enforcement. To meet extreme or flagrant violations all forms of judicial enforcement must be made available.

The commission proposed is new and will be materially different from the NRA. Its powers will be less drastic and yet adequate to accomplish its objectives. In structure and action it will be in harmony with constitutional principles. It should stimulate and maintain widespread coöperation of trade and industry. It should work in close contact with trade associations in the industries. Planned to be permanent in form, its name should so indicate. National Industrial Administration might be deemed appropriate.

For necessary and effective judicial control of the new industrial commission it would seem advisable to create by Act of Congress a special court having jurisdiction of appeals from all decisions of the new commission approving codes or imposing rules or regulations on industry. Such a court would resemble the Commerce Court which had a brief but not inglorious career. It would insure a tribunal composed of judges of special training and experience qualified to determine the conflicts between government and industry which will arise in the administration of the new statute. It would also insure expedition in the hearing and decision of appeals. Its most important function will be the judicial review of an order imposing a compulsory code. It should have original jurisdiction over all controversies in which it is claimed by any citizen that the code or regulation violates any principle of the Constitution and destroys or irreparably injures business or property. The concurrent jurisdiction of all courts to enforce compliance with codes should be reserved.

These venturous suggestions may, perhaps, point to some of the distinguishing features of the new plan of regulation to succeed the NRA. The new plan, however devised, will also be an experiment. Any scheme of government for the regulation of the activities of merchants and manufacturers must perforce be an experiment subject to changes through experience. The new statute will also be a compromise. It will be a compromise between individual freedom of action and regulation by government. In the development and application of its powers over trade and industry it may gradually realize upon a working basis that aspiration of the Supreme Court, a rational compromise between individual rights and public welfare. The sum of all its activities will be another search of a democratic society *for the ideal of justice in human relations.*

APPENDIX I

THE PRESIDENT'S MESSAGE

To the Congress:

Before the special session of the Congress adjourns, I recommend two further steps in our national campaign to put people to work.

My first request is that (I) the Congress provide for the machinery necessary for a great cooperative movement throughout all industry in order to obtain wide re-employment, to shorten the work week, to pay a decent wage for the shorter week and *to prevent unfair competition and disastrous overproduction.*

Employers cannot do this singly or even in organized groups, because such action increases costs and thus permits cutthroat underselling by selfish competitors unwilling to join in such a public-spirited endeavor.

One of the great restrictions upon such cooperative efforts up to this time has been our anti-trust laws. They were properly designed as the means to cure the great evils of monopolistic price fixing. They should certainly be retained as a permanent assurance that the old evils of unfair competition shall never return. But the public interest will be served if, with the authority and under the guidance of government, private industries are permitted to make agreements and codes insuring fair competition. However, it is necessary, if we thus limit the operation of anti-trust laws to their original purpose, to provide a rigorous licensing power in order to meet rare cases of non-cooperation and abuse. Such a safeguard is indispensable.

The other proposal (II) gives the Executive full power to start a large program of direct employment. A careful survey convinces me that approximately $3,300,000,000 can be invested in useful and necessary public construction, and at the same time put the largest possible number of people to work.

Provision should be made to permit States, counties and municipalities to undertake useful public works, subject, however, to the most effective possible means of eliminating favoritism and wasteful expenditures on unwarranted and uneconomic projects.

We must, by prompt and vigorous action, override unnecessary obstructions which in the past have delayed the starting of public works programs. This can be accomplished by simple and direct procedure.

In carrying out this program it is imperative that the credit of the United States Government be protected and preserved. This means that at the same time we are making these vast emergency expenditures there must be provided sufficient revenue to pay interest and amortization on the cost and that the revenues so provided must be adequate and certain rather than inadequate and speculative.

Careful estimates indicate that at least $220,000,000 of additional revenue will be required to service the contemplated borrowing of the government. This will of necessity involve some form or forms of new taxation. A number of suggestions have been made as to the nature of these taxes.

I do not make a specific recommendation at this time, but I hope that the Committee of Ways and Means of the House of Representatives will make a careful study of revenue plans and be prepared by the beginning of the coming week to propose the taxes which they judge to be best adapted to meet the present need and which will at the same time be least burdensome to our people. At the end of that time, if no decision has been reached or if the means proposed do not seem to be sufficiently adequate or certain, it is my intention to transmit to the Congress my own recommendations in the matter.

The taxes to be imposed are for the purpose of providing re-employment for our citizens. Provision should be made for their reduction or elimination—

First—As fast as increasing revenues from improving business become available to replace them;

Second—Whenever the repeal of the Eighteenth Amendment now pending before the States shall have been ratified and the repeal of the Volstead act effected. The pre-prohibition revenue laws would then automatically go into effect and yield enough wholly to eliminate these temporary re-employment taxes.

Finally, I stress the fact that all of these proposals are based on the gravity of the emergency and that, therefore, it is urgently necessary immediately to initiate a re-employment campaign if we are to avoid further hardships, to sustain business improvement and to pass on to better things.

For this reason I urge prompt action on this legislation.

FRANKLIN D. ROOSEVELT

The White House, May 17, 1933

APPENDIX II

THE NATIONAL INDUSTRIAL RECOVERY ACT
as Passed by Congress, June 13, 1933

73D CONGRESS, 1ST SESSION

(H. R. 5755)

AN ACT

To encourage national industrial recovery, to foster fair competition, and to provide for the construction of certain useful public works, and for other purposes.

Be it enacted by the Senate and House of Representatives of the United States of America in Congress assembled,

TITLE I—INDUSTRIAL RECOVERY

DECLARATION OF POLICY

SECTION 1. A national emergency productive of widespread unemployment and disorganization of industry, which burdens interstate and foreign commerce, affects the public welfare, and undermines the standards of living of the American people, is hereby declared to exist. It is hereby declared to be the policy of Congress to remove obstructions to the free flow of interstate and foreign commerce which tend to diminish the amount thereof; and to provide for the general welfare by promoting the organization of industry for the purpose of cooperative action among trade groups, to induce and maintain united action of labor and management under adequate governmental sanctions and supervision, to eliminate unfair competitive practices, to promote the fullest possible utilization of the present productive capacity of industries, to avoid undue restriction of production (except as may be temporarily required), to increase the consumption of industrial and agricultural products by increasing purchasing power, to reduce and relieve unemployment, to improve standards of labor, and otherwise to rehabilitate industry and to conserve natural resources.

ADMINISTRATIVE AGENCIES

SEC. 2. (*a*) To effectuate the policy of this title, the President is hereby authorized to establish such agencies, to accept and utilize such voluntary and uncompensated services, to appoint, without regard to the provisions of the civil service laws, such officers and employees, and to utilize such Federal officers and employees, and, with the consent of the State, such State and local officers and employees, as he may find necessary, to prescribe their authorities, duties, responsibilities, and tenure, and, without regard to the Classification Act of 1923, as amended, to fix the compensation of any officers and employees so appointed.

(*b*) The President may delegate any of his functions and powers under this title to such officers, agents, and employees as he may designate or appoint, and may establish an industrial planning and research agency to aid in carrying out his functions under this title.

(*c*) This title shall cease to be in effect and any agencies established hereunder shall cease to exist at the expiration of two years after the date of enactment of this Act, or sooner if the President shall by proclamation or the Congress shall by joint resolution declare that the emergency recognized by section 1 has ended.

CODES OF FAIR COMPETITION

SEC. 3. (*a*) Upon the application to the President by one or more trade or industrial associations or groups, the President may approve a code or codes of fair competition for the trade or industry or subdivision thereof, represented by the applicant or applicants, if the President finds (1) that such associations or groups impose no inequitable restrictions on admission to membership therein and are truly representative of such trades or industries or subdivisions thereof, and (2) that such code or codes are not designed to promote monopolies or to eliminate or oppress small enterprises and will not operate to discriminate against them, and will tend to effectuate the policy of this title: *Provided,* That such code or codes shall not permit monopolies or monopolistic practices: *Provided further,* That where such code or codes affect the services and welfare of persons engaged in other steps of the economic process, nothing in this section shall deprive such persons of the right to be heard prior to approval by the President of such code or codes. The President may, as a condition of his approval of any such code, impose such conditions (including requirements for the making of reports and the keeping of accounts) for the protection of consumers, competitors, employees, and others, and in furtherance of the public interest, and may provide such exceptions to and exemptions from the provisions of such code, as the President in his discretion deems necessary to effectuate the policy herein declared.

(*b*) After the President shall have approved any such code, the provisions of such code shall be the standards of fair competition for such trade or industry or subdivision thereof. Any violation of such standards in any transaction in or affecting interstate or foreign commerce shall be deemed an unfair method of competition in commerce within the meaning of the Federal Trade Commission Act, as amended; but nothing in this title shall be construed to impair the powers of the Federal Trade Commission under such Act, as amended.

(*c*) The several district courts of the United States are hereby invested with jurisdiction to prevent and restrain violations of any code of fair competition approved under this title; and it shall be the duty of the several district attorneys of the United States, in their respective districts, under the direction of the Attorney General, to institute proceedings in equity to prevent and restrain such violations.

(*d*) Upon his own motion, or if complaint is made to the President that abuses inimical to the public interest and contrary to the policy herein declared are prevalent in any trade or industry or subdivision thereof, and if no code of fair competition therefor has theretofore been approved by the President, the President, after such public notice and hearing as he shall specify, may prescribe and approve a code of fair competition for such trade or industry or subdivision thereof, which shall have the same effect as a code of fair competition approved by the President under subsection (a) of this section.

(*e*) On his own motion, or if any labor organization, or any trade or industrial organization, association, or group, which has complied with the provisions of this title, shall make complaint to the President that any article or articles are being imported into the United States in substantial quantities or increasing ratio to domestic production of any competitive article or articles and on such terms or under such conditions as to render ineffective or seriously to endanger the maintenance of any code or agreement under this title, the President may cause an immediate investigation to be made by the United States Tariff Commission, which shall give precedence to investigations under this subsection, and if, after such investigation and such public notice and hearing as he shall specify, the President shall find the existence of such facts, he shall in order to effectuate the policy of this title, direct that the article or articles concerned shall be permitted entry into the United States only upon such terms and conditions and subject to the payment of such fees and to such limitations in the total quantity which may be imported (in the course of any specified period or periods) as he shall find it necessary to prescribe in order that the entry thereof shall not render or tend to render ineffective any code or agreement made under this title. In order to enforce any limitations imposed on the total quantity of imports, in any specified period or periods, of any article or articles under this subsection, the President may forbid the importation of such article or articles unless the importer shall have first obtained from the Secretary of the Treasury a license pursuant to such regulations as the President may prescribe. Upon information of any action by the President under this subsection the Secretary of the Treasury shall, through the proper officers, permit entry of the article or articles specified only upon such terms and conditions and subject to such fees, to such limitations in the quantity which may be imported, and to such requirements of license, as the President shall have directed. The decision of the President as to facts shall be conclusive. Any condition or limitation of entry under this subsection shall continue in effect until the President shall find and inform the Secretary of the Treasury that the conditions which led to the imposition of such condition or limitation upon entry no longer exists.

(*f*) When a code of fair competition has been approved or prescribed by the President under this title, any violation of any provision thereof in any transaction in or affecting interstate or foreign commerce shall be a misdemeanor and upon conviction thereof an offender shall be fined not more than $500 for each offense, and each day such violation continues shall be deemed a separate offense.

AGREEMENTS AND LICENSES

SEC. 4. (*a*) The President is authorized to enter into agreements with, and to approve voluntary agreements between and among, persons engaged in a trade or industry, labor organizations, and trade or industrial organizations, associations, or groups, relating to any trade or industry, if in his judgment such agreements will aid in effectuating the policy of this title with respect to transactions in or affecting interstate or foreign commerce, and will be consistent with the requirements of clause (2) of subsection (*a*) of section 3 for a code of fair competition.

(*b*) Whenever the President shall find that destructive wage or price cutting or other activities contrary to the policy of this title are being practiced in any trade or industry or any subdivision thereof, and, after such public notice and hearing as he shall specify, shall find it essential to license business enterprises in order to make effective a code of fair competition or an agreement under this title or otherwise to effectuate the policy of this title, and shall publicly so announce, no person shall, after a date fixed in such announcement, engage in or carry on any business, in or affecting interstate or foreign commerce, specified in such announcement, unless he shall have first obtained a license issued pursuant to such regulations as the President shall prescribe. The President may suspend or revoke any such license, after due notice and opportunity for hearing, for violations of the terms or conditions thereof. Any order of the President suspending or revoking any such license shall be final if in accordance with law. Any person who, without such a license or in violation of any condition thereof, carries on any such business for which a license is so required, shall, upon conviction thereof, be fined not more than $500, or imprisoned not more than six months, or both, and each day such violation continues shall be deemed a separate offense. Notwithstanding the provisions of section 2 (*c*), this subsection shall cease to be in effect at the expiration of one year after the date of enactment of this Act or sooner if the President shall by proclamation or the Congress shall by joint resolution declare that the emergency recognized by section 1 has ended.

SEC. 5. While this title is in effect (or in the case of a license, while section 4 (*a*) is in effect) and for sixty days thereafter, any code, agreement, or license approved, prescribed, or issued and in effect under this title, and any action complying with the provisions thereof taken during such period, shall be exempt from the provisions of the anti-trust laws of the United States.

Nothing in this Act, and no regulation thereunder, shall prevent an individual from pursuing the vocation of manual labor and selling or trading the products thereof; nor shall anything in this Act, or regulation thereunder, prevent anyone from marketing or trading the produce of his farm.

LIMITATIONS UPON APPLICATION OF TITLE

SEC. 6. (*a*) No trade or industrial association or group shall be eligible to receive the benefit of the provisions of this title until it files with the President a statement containing such information relating to the activities of the association or group as the President shall by regulation prescribe.

(*b*) The President is authorized to prescribe rules and regulations designed to insure that any organization availing itself of the benefits of this title shall be truly representative of the trade or industry or subdivision thereof represented by such organization. Any organization violating any such rule or regulation shall cease to be entitled to the benefits of this title.

(*c*) Upon the request of the President, the Federal Trade

Commission shall make such investigations as may be necessary to enable the President to carry out the provisions of this title, and for such purposes the Commission shall have all the powers vested in it with respect to investigations under the Federal Trade Commission Act, as amended.

SEC. 7. (*a*) Every code of fair competition, agreement, and license approved, prescribed, or issued under this title shall contain the following conditions: (1) That employees shall have the right to organize and bargain collectively through representatives of their own choosing, and shall be free from the interference, restraint, or coercion of employers of labor, or their agents, in the designation of such representatives or in self-organization or in other concerted activities for the purpose of collective bargaining or other mutual aid or protection; (2) that no employee and no one seeking employment shall be required as a condition of employment to join any company union or to refrain from joining, organizing, or assisting a labor organization of his own choosing; and (3) that employers shall comply with the maximum hours of labor, minimum rates of pay, and other conditions of employment, approved or prescribed by the President.

(*b*) The President shall, so far as practicable, afford every opportunity to employers and employees in any trade or industry or subdivision thereof with respect to which the conditions referred to in clauses (1) and (2) of subsection (a) prevail, to establish by mutual agreement, the standards as to the maximum hours of labor, minimum rates of pay, and such other conditions of employment as may be necessary in such trade or industry or subdivision thereof to effectuate the policy of this title; and the standards established in such agreements, when approved by the President, shall have the same effect as a code of fair competition, approved by the President under subsection (*a*) of section 3.

(*c*) Where no such mutual agreement has been approved by the President he may investigate the labor practices, policies, wages, hours of labor, and conditions of employment in such trade or industry or subdivision thereof; and upon the basis of such investigations, and after such hearings as the President finds advisable, he is authorized to prescribe a limited code of fair competition fixing such maximum hours of labor, minimum rates of pay, and other conditions of employment in the trade or industry or subdivision thereof investigated as he finds to be necessary to effectuate the policy of this title, which shall have the same effect as a code of fair competition approved by the President under subsection (*a*) of section 3. The President may differentiate according to experience and skill of the employees affected and according to the locality of employment; but no attempt shall be made to introduce any classification according to the nature of the work involved which might tend to set a maximum as well as a minimum wage.

(*d*) As used in this title, the term "person" includes any individual, partnership, association, trust, or corporation; and the terms "interstate and foreign commerce" and "interstate or foreign commerce" include, except where otherwise indicated, trade or commerce among the several States and with foreign nations, or between the District of Columbia or any Territory of the United States and any State, Territory, or foreign nation, or between any insular possessions or other places under the jurisdiction of the United States, or between any such possession or place and any State or Territory of the United States or the District of Columbia or any foreign nation, or within the District of Columbia or any Territory or any insular possession or other place under the jurisdiction of the United States.

APPLICATION OF AGRICULTURAL ADJUSTMENT ACT

SEC. 8. (*a*) This title shall not be construed to repeal or modify any of the provisions of title I of the Act entitled "An Act to relieve the existing national economic emergency by increasing agricultural purchasing power, to raise revenue for extraordinary expenses incurred by reason of such emergency, to provide emergency relief with respect to agricultural indebtedness, to provide for the orderly liquidation of joint-stock land banks, and for other purposes," approved May 12, 1933; and such title I of said Act approved May 12, 1933, may for all purposes be hereafter referred to as the "Agricultural Adjustment Act."

(*b*) The President may, in his discretion, in order to avoid conflicts in the administration of the Agricultural Adjustment Act and this title, delegate any of his functions and powers under this title with respect to trades, industries, or subdivisions thereof which are engaged in the handling of any agricultural commodity or product thereof, or of any competing commodity or product thereof, to the Secretary of Agriculture.

OIL REGULATION

SEC. 9. (*a*) The President is further authorized to initiate before the Interstate Commerce proceedings necessary to prescribe regulations to control the operations of oil pipe lines and to fix reasonable, compensatory rates for the transportation of petroleum and its products by pipe lines, and the Interstate Commerce Commission shall grant preference to the hearings and determination of such cases.

(*b*) The President is authorized to institute proceedings to divorce from any holding company any pipe-line company controlled by such holding company which pipe-line company by unfair practices or by exorbitant rates in the transportation of petroleum or its products tends to create a monopoly.

(*c*) The President is authorized to prohibit the transportation in interstate and foreign commerce of petroleum and the products thereof produced or withdrawn from storage in excess of the amount permitted to be produced or withdrawn from storage by any State law or valid regulation or order prescribed thereunder, by any board, commission, officer, or other duly authorized agency of a State. Any violation of any order of the President issued under the provisions of this subsection shall be punishable by fine of not to exceed $1,000, or imprisonment for not to exceed six months, or both.

RULES AND REGULATIONS

SEC. 10. (*a*) The President is authorized to prescribe such rules and regulations as may be necessary to carry out the purposes of this title, and fees for licenses and for filing codes of fair competition and agreements, and any violation of any such rule or regulation shall be punishable by fine of not to exceed $500, or imprisonment for not to exceed six months, or both.

(*b*) The President may from time to time cancel or modify any order, approval, license, rule, or regulation issued under this title; and each agreement, code of fair competition, or license approved, prescribed, or issued under this title shall contain an express provision to that effect.

TITLE II—PUBLIC WORKS AND CONSTRUCTION PROJECTS

FEDERAL EMERGENCY ADMINISTRATION OF PUBLIC WORKS

SECTION 201. (*a*) To effectuate the purposes of this title, the President is hereby authorized to create a Federal Emergency Administration of Public Works, all the powers of which shall be exercised by a Federal Emergency Administrator of Public Works (hereafter referred to as the "Administrator"), and to establish such agencies, to accept and utilize such voluntary and uncompensated services, to appoint, without regard to the civil service laws, such officers and employees, and to utilize such Federal officers and employees, and, with the consent of the State, such State and local officers and employees as he may find necessary, to prescribe their authorities, duties, responsibilities, and tenure, and, without regard to the Classification Act of 1923, as amended, to fix the compensation of any officers and employees so appointed. The President may delegate any of his functions and powers under this title to such officers, agents, and employees as he may designate or appoint.

(*b*) The Administrator may, without regard to the civil service laws or the Classification Act of 1923, as amended, appoint and fix the compensation of such experts and such other officers and employees as are necessary to carry out the provisions of this title; and may make such expenditures (including expenditures for personal services and rent at the seat of government and elsewhere, for law books and books of reference, and for paper, printing and binding) as are necessary to carry out the provisions of this title.

(*c*) All such compensation, expenses, and allowances shall be paid out of funds made available by this Act.

(*d*) After the expiration of two years after the date of the enactment of this Act, or sooner if the President shall by proclamation or the Congress shall by joint resolution declare that the emergency recognized by section 1 has ended, the President shall not make any further loans or grants or enter upon any new construction under this title, and any agencies established hereunder shall cease to exist and any of their remaining functions shall be transferred to such departments of the Government as the President shall designate: *Provided,* That he may issue funds to a borrower under this title prior to January 23, 1939, under the terms of any agreement, or any commitment to bid upon or purchase bonds, entered into with such borrower prior to the date of termination, under this section, of the power of the President to make loans.

SEC. 202. The Administrator, under the direction of the President, shall prepare a comprehensive program of public works, which shall include among other things the following: (*a*) Construction, repair, and improvement of public highways and parkways, public buildings, and any publicly owned instrumentalities and facilities; (*b*) conservation and development of natural resources, including control, utilization, and purification of waters, prevention of soil on coastal erosion, development of water power, transmission of electrical energy, and construction of river and harbor improvements and flood control, and also the construction of any river or drainage improvement required to perform or satisfy any obligation incurred by the United States through a treaty with a foreign Government heretofore ratified and to restore or develop for the use of any State or its citizens water taken from or denied to them by performance on the part of the United States of treaty obligations heretofore assumed: Provided, that no river or harbor improvements shall be carried out unless they shall have heretofore or hereafter been adopted by the Congress or are recommended by the Chief of Engineers of the United States Army; (*c*) any projects of the character heretofore constructed or carried on either directly by public authority or with public aid to serve the interests of the general public; (*d*) construction, reconstruction, alteration, or repair under public regulation or control of low-cost housing and slum-clearance projects; (*e*) any project (other than those included in the foregoing classes) of any character heretofore eligible for loans under subsection (*a*) of section 201 of the Emergency Relief and Construction Act of 1932, as amended, and paragraph (3) of such subsection (*a*) shall for such purposes be held to include loans for the construction or completion of hospitals the operation of which is partly financed from public funds, and of reservoirs and pumping plants and for the construction of dry docks; and if in the opinion of the President it seems desirable, the construction of naval vessels within the terms and/or limits established by the London Naval Treaty of 1930 and of aircraft required therefor and construction of heavier-than-air aircraft and technical construction for the Army Air Corps and such Army housing projects as the President may approve, and provision of original equipment for the mechanization or motorization of such Army tactical units as he may designate: *Provided, however,* That in the event of an international agreement for the further limitation of armament, to which the United States is signatory, the President is hereby authorized and empowered to suspend, in whole or in part, any such naval or military construction or mechanization and motorization of Army units: *Provided, further,* That this title shall not be applicable to public works under the jurisdiction or control of the Architect of the Capitol or of any commission or committee for which such Architect is the contracting and/or executive officer.

Sec. 203. (*a*) With a view to increasing employment quickly (while reasonably securing any loans made by the United States) the President is authorized and empowered, through the Administrator or through such other agencies as he may designate or create, (1) to construct, finance, or aid in the construction or financing of any public works project included in the program prepared pursuant to section 202; (2) upon such terms as the President shall prescribe, to make grants to States, municipalities, or other public bodies for the construction, repair, or improvement of any such project, but no such grant shall be in excess of 30 per centum of the cost of the labor and materials employed upon such subject; (3) to acquire by purchase, or by exercise of the power of eminent domain, any real or personal property in connection with the construction of any such project, and to sell any security acquired or any property so constructed or acquired or to lease any such property with or without the privilege of purchase: *Provided,* That all moneys received from any such sale or lease or the repayment of any loan shall be used to retire obligations issued pursuant to section 209 of this Act, in addition to any other moneys required to be used for such purpose; (4) to aid in the financing of such railroad maintenance and equipment as may be approved by the Interstate Commerce Commission as desirable for the improvement of transportation facilities; and (5) to advance, upon request of the Commission having jurisdiction of the project, the unappropriated balance of the sum authorized for carrying out the provisions of the Act entitled "An Act to provide for the construction and equipment of an annex to the Library of Congress," approved June 13, 1930 (46 Stat. 583); such advance to be expended under the direction of such Commission and in accordance with such Act: *Provided,* That in deciding to extend any aid or grant hereunder to any State, county, or municipality the President may consider whether action is in process or in good faith assured therein reasonably designed to bring the ordinary current expenditures thereof within the prudently estimated revenues thereof. The provisions of this section and section 202 shall extend to public works in the several States, Hawaii, Alaska, the District of Columbia, Puerto Rico, the Canal Zone, and the Virgin Islands.

(*b*) All expenditures for authorized travel by officers and employees, including subsistence, required on account of any Federal public-works projects, shall be charged to the amounts allocated to such projects, notwithstanding any other provisions of law; and there is authorized to be employed such personal services in the District of Columbia and elsewhere as may be required to be engaged upon such work and to be in addition to employees otherwise provided for, the compensation of such additional personal services to be a charge against the funds made available for such construction work.

(*c*) In the acquisition of any land or site for the purposes of Federal public buildings and in the construction of such buildings provided for in this title, the provisions contained in sections 305 and 306 of the Emergency Relief and Construction Act of 1932, as amended, shall apply.

(*d*) The President, in his discretion, and under such terms as he may prescribe, may extend any of the benefits of this title to any State, county, or municipality notwithstanding any constitutional or legal restriction or limitation on the right or power of such State, county, or municipality to borrow money or incur indebtedness.

SEC. 204. (*a*) For the purpose of providing for emergency construction of public highways and related projects, the President is authorized to make grants to the highway departments of the several States in an amount not less than $400,000,000, to be expended by such departments in accordance with the provisions of the Federal Highway Act, approved November 9, 1921, as amended and supplemented, except as provided in this title, as follows:

(1) For expenditure in emergency construction on the Federal aid highway system and extensions thereof into and through municipalities. The amount apportioned to any State under this paragraph may be used to pay all or any part of the cost of surveys, plans, and of highway and bridge construction including the elimination of hazards to highway traffic, such as the separation of grades at crossings, the reconstruction of existing railroad grade crossing structures, the relocation of highways to eliminate railroad crossings, the widening of narrow bridges and roadways, the building of footpaths, the replacement of unsafe bridges, the construction of routes to avoid congested areas, the construction of facilities to improve accessibility and the free flow of traffic, and the cost of any other construction that will provide safer traffic facilities or definitely eliminate existing hazards to pedestrian or vehicular traffic. No funds made available

by this title shall be used for the acquisition of any land, right of way, or easement in connection with any railroad grade elimination project.

(2) For expenditure in emergency construction on secondary or feeder roads to be agreed upon by the State highway departments and the Secretary of Agriculture: *Provided,* That the State or responsible political subdivision shall provide for the proper maintenance of said roads. Such grants shall be available for payment of the full cost of surveys, plans, improvement, and construction of secondary or feeder roads, on which projects shall be submitted by the State highway department and approved by the Secretary of Agriculture.

(*b*) Any amounts allocated by the President for grants under subsection (*a*) of this section shall be apportioned among the several States, seven-eighths in accordance with the provisions of section 21 of the Federal Highway Act, approved November 9, 1921, as amended and supplemented (which Act is hereby further amended for the purposes of this title to include the District of Columbia), and one-eighth in the ratio which the population of each State bears to the total population of the United States, according to the latest decennial census, and shall be available on July 1, 1933, and shall remain available until expended; but no part of the funds apportioned to any State need be matched by the State, and such funds may also be used in lieu of State funds to match unobligated balances of previous apportionments of regular Federal-aid appropriations.

(*c*) All contracts involving the expenditure of such grants shall contain provisions establishing minimum rates of wages, to be predetermined by the State highway department, which contractors shall pay to skilled and unskilled labor, and such minimum rates shall be stated in the invitation for bids and shall be included in proposals for bids for the work.

(*d*) In the expenditure of such amounts, the limitations in the Federal Highway Act, approved November 9, 1921, as amended and supplemented, upon highway construction, reconstruction, and bridges within municipalities and upon payments per mile which may be made from Federal funds, shall not apply.

(*e*) As used in this section the term "State" includes the Territory of Hawaii and the District of Columbia. The term "highway" as defined in the Federal Highway Act approved November 9, 1921, as amended and supplemented, for the purposes of this section, shall be deemed to include such main parkways as may be designated by the State and approved by the Secretary of Agriculture as part of the Federal-aid highway system.

(*f*) Whenever, in connection with the construction of any highway project under this section or section 202 of this Act, it is necessary to acquire rights of way over or through any property or tracts of land owned and controlled by the Government of the United States, it shall be the duty of the proper official of the Government of the United States having control of such property or tracts of land with the approval of the President and the Attorney General of the United States, and without any expense whatsoever to the United States, to perform any acts and to execute any agreements necessary to grant the rights of way so required, but if at any time the land or the property the subject of the agreement shall cease to be used for the purposes of the highway, the title in and the jurisdiction over the land or property shall automatically revert to the Government of the United States and the agreement shall so provide.

(*g*) Hereafter in the administration of the Federal Highway Act, and Acts amendatory thereof or supplementary thereto, the first paragraph of section 9 of said Act shall not apply to publicly owned toll bridges or approaches thereto, operated by the highway department of any State, subject, however, to the condition that all tolls received from the operation of any such bridge, less the actual cost of operation and maintenance, shall be applied to the repayment of the cost of its construction or acquisition, and when the cost of its construction or acquisition shall have been repaid in full, such bridge thereafter shall be maintained and operated as a free bridge.

SEC. 205. (*a*) Not less than $50,000,000 of the amount made available by this Act shall be allotted for (A) national forest highways, (B) national forest roads, trails, bridges, and related projects, (C) national park roads and trails in national parks owned or authorized, (D) roads on Indian reservations, and (E) roads through public lands, to be expended in the same manner as provided in paragraph (2) of section 301 of the Emergency Relief and Construction Act of 1932, in the case of appropriations allocated for such purposes, respectively, in such section 301, to remain available until expended.

(*b*) The President may also allot funds made available by this Act for the construction, repair, and improvement of public highways in Alaska, the Canal Zone, Puerto Rico, and the Virgin Islands.

SEC. 206. All contracts let for construction projects and all loans and grants pursuant to this title shall contain such provisions as are necessary to insure (1) that no convict labor shall be employed on any such project; (2) that (except in executive, administrative, and supervisory positions), so far as practicable and feasible, no individual directly employed on any such project shall be permitted to work more than thirty hours in any one week; (3) that all employees shall be paid just and reasonable wages which shall be compensation sufficient to provide, for the hours of labor as limited, a standard of living in decency and comfort; (4) that in the employment of labor in connection with any such project, preference shall be given, where they are qualified, to ex-service men with dependents, and then in the following order: (A) To citizens of the United States and aliens, who have declared their intention of becoming citizens, who are bona fide residents of the political subdivision and/or county in which the work is to be performed, and (B) to citizens of the United States and aliens who have declared their intention of becoming citizens, who are bona fide residents of the State, Territory, or District in which the work is to be performed: *Provided,* That these preferences shall apply only where such labor is available and qualified to perform the work to which the employment relates; and (5) that the maximum of human labor shall be used in lieu of machinery wherever practicable and consistent with sound economy and public advantage.

SEC. 207. (*a*) For the purpose of expediting the actual construction of public works contemplated by this title and to provide a means of financial assistance to persons under contract with the United States to perform such construction, the President is authorized and empowered, through the Administrator or through such other agencies as he may designate or create, to approve any assignment executed by any such contractor, with the written consent of the surety or sureties upon the penal bond executed in connection with his contract, to any national or State bank, or his claim against the United States, or any part of such claim, under such contract; and any assignment so approved shall be valid for all purposes, notwithstanding the provisions of sections 3737 and 3477 of the Revised Statutes, as amended.

(*b*) The funds received by a contractor under any advances made in consideration of any such assignment are hereby declared to be trust funds in the hands of such contractors to be first applied to the payment of claims of subcontractors, architects, engineers, surveyors, laborers, and material men in connection with the project, to the payment of premiums on the penal bond or bonds, and premiums accruing during the construction of such project on insurance policies taken in connection therewith. Any contractor and any officer, director, or agent of any such contractor, who applies, or consents to the application of, such funds for any other purpose and fails to pay any claim or premium hereinbefore mentioned, shall be deemed guilty of a misdemeanor and shall be punished by a fine of not more than $1,000 or by imprisonment for not more than one year, or by both such fine and imprisonment.

(*c*) Nothing in this section shall be considered as imposing upon the assignee any obligation to see to the proper application of the funds advanced by the assignee in consideration of such assignment.

SUBSISTENCE HOMESTEADS

SEC. 208. To provide for aiding the redistribution of the over-balance of population in industrial centers $25,000,000 is hereby made available to the President, to be used by him through such agencies as he may establish and under such regulations as he may make, for making loans for and otherwise aiding in the purchase of subsistence homesteads. The moneys collected as repayment of said loans shall constitute a revolving fund to be administered as directed by the President for the purposes of this section.

RULES AND REGULATIONS

SEC. 209. The President is authorized to prescribe such rules and regulations as may be necessary to carry out the purposes of this title, and any violation of any such rule or regulation shall be punishable by fine of not to exceed $500 or imprisonment not to exceed six months, or both.

ISSUE OF SECURITIES AND SINKING FUND

SEC. 210. (*a*) The Secretary of the Treasury is authorized to borrow, from time to time, under the Second Liberty Bond Act, as amended, such amounts as may be necessary to meet the expenditures authorized by this Act, or to refund any obligations previously issued under this section, and to issue therefor bonds, notes, certificates of indebtedness, or Treasury bills of the United States.

(*b*) For each fiscal year beginning with the fiscal year 1934 there is hereby appropriated, in addition to and as part of, the cumulative sinking fund provided by section 6 of the Victory Liberty Loan Act, as amended, out of any money in the Treasury not otherwise appropriated, for the purpose of such fund, an amount equal to 2½ per centum of the aggregate amount of the expenditures made out of appropriations made or authorized under this Act as determined by the Secretary of the Treasury.

REEMPLOYMENT AND RELIEF TAXES

SEC. 211. (*a*) Effective as of the day following the date of the enactment of this Act, section 617 (a) of the Revenue Act of 1932 is amended by striking out "1 cent" and inserting in lieu thereof "1½ cents."

(*b*) Effective as of the day following the date of the enactment of this Act, section 617 (*c*) (2) of such Act is amended by adding at the end thereof a new sentence to read as follows: "As used in this paragraph the term 'benzol' does not include benzol sold for use otherwise than as a fuel for the propulsion of motor vehicles, motor boats, or airplanes, and otherwise than in the manufacture or production of such fuel."

SEC. 212. Titles IV and V of the Revenue Act of 1932 are amended by striking out "1934" wherever appearing therein and by inserting in lieu thereof "1935." Section 761 of the Revenue Act of 1932 is further amended by striking out "and on July 1, 1933" and inserting in lieu thereof "and on July 1, 1933, and on July 1, 1934."

SEC. 213. (*a*) There is hereby imposed upon the receipt of dividends (required to be included in the gross income of the recipient under the provisions of the Revenue Act of 1932) by any person other than a domestic corporation, an excise tax equal to 5 per centum of the amount thereof, such tax to be deducted and withheld from such dividends by the payor corporation. The tax imposed by this section shall not apply to dividends declared before the date of the enactment of this Act.

(*b*) Every corporation required to deduct and withhold any tax under this section shall, on or before the last day of the month following the payment of the dividend, make return thereof and pay the tax to the collector of the district in which its principal place of business is located, or, if it has no principal place of business in the United States, to the collector at Baltimore, Maryland.

(*c*) Every such corporation is hereby made liable for such tax and is hereby indemnified against the claims and demands of any person for the amount of any payment in accordance with the provisions of this section.

(*d*) The provisions of sections 115, 771 to 774, inclusive, and 1111 of the Revenue Act of 1932 shall be applicable with respect to the tax imposed by this section.

(*e*) The taxes imposed by this section shall not apply to

the dividends of any corporation enumerated in section 103 of the Revenue Act of 1932.

SEC. 214. Section 104 of the Revenue Act of 1932 is amended by striking out the words "the surtax" wherever occurring in such section and inserting in lieu thereof "any internal-revenue tax." The heading of such section is amended by striking out "surtaxes" and inserting in lieu thereof "internal-revenue taxes." Section 13 (*c*) of such Act is amended by striking out "surtax" and inserting in lieu thereof "internal-revenue tax."

SEC. 215. (*a*) For each year ending June 30 there is hereby imposed upon every domestic corporation with respect to carrying on or doing business for any part of such year an excise tax of $1 for each $1,000 of the adjusted declared value of its capital stock.

(*b*) For each year ending June 30 there is hereby imposed upon every foreign corporation with respect to carrying on or doing business in the United States for any part of such year an excise tax equivalent to $1 for each $1,000 of the adjusted declared value of capital employed in the transaction of its business in the United States.

(*c*) The taxes imposed by this section shall not apply—

(1) to any corporation enumerated in section 103 of the Revenue Act of 1932;

(2) to any insurance company subject to the tax imposed by section 201 or 204 of such Act;

(3) to any domestic corporation in respect of the year ending June 30, 1933, if it did not carry on or do business during a part of the period from the date of the enactment of this Act to June 30, 1933, both dates inclusive; or

(4) to any foreign corporation in respect of the year ending June 30, 1933, if it did not carry on or do business in the United States during a part of the period from the date of the enactment of this Act to June 30, 1933, both dates inclusive.

(*d*) Every corporation liable for tax under this section shall make a return under oath within one month after the close of the year with respect to which such tax is imposed to the collector for the district in which is located its principal place of business or, if it has no principal place of business in the United States, then to the collector at Baltimore, Maryland. Such return shall contain such information and be made in such manner as the Commissioner with the approval of the Secretary may by regulations prescribe. The tax shall, without assessment by the Commissioner or notice from the collector, be due and payable to the collector before the expiration of the period for filing the return. If the tax is not paid when due, there shall be added as part of the tax interest at the rate of 1 per centum a month from the time when the tax became due until paid. All provisions of law (including penalties) applicable in respect of the taxes imposed by section 600 of the Revenue Act of 1926 shall, insofar as not inconsistent with this section, be applicable in respect of the taxes imposed by this section. The Commissioner may extend the time for making the returns and paying the taxes imposed by this section, under such rules and regulations as he may prescribe with the approval of the Secretary, but no such extension shall be for more than sixty days.

(*e*) Returns required to be filed for the purpose of the tax imposed by this section shall be open to inspection in the same manner, to the same extent, and subject to the same provisions of law, including penalties, as returns made under title II of the Revenue Act of 1926.

(*f*) For the first year ending June 30 in respect of which a tax is imposed by this section upon any corporation, the adjusted declared value shall be the value, as declared by the corporation in its first return under this section (which declaration of value cannot be amended), as of the close of its last income-tax taxable year ending at or prior to the close of the year for which the tax is imposed by this section (or as of the date of organization in the case of a corporation having no income-tax taxable year ending at or prior to the close of the year for which the tax is imposed by this section). For any subsequent year ending June 30, the adjusted declared value in the case of a domestic corporation shall be the original declared value plus (1) the cash and fair market value of property paid in for stock or shares, (2) paid-in surplus and contributions to capital, and (3) earnings and profits, and minus (A) the value of property distributed in liquidation to shareholders, (B) distributions of earnings and profits, and (C) deficits, whether operating or nonoperating; each adjustment being made for the period from the date as of which the original declared value was declared to the close of its last income-tax taxable year ending at or prior to the close of the year for which the tax is imposed by this section. For any subsequent year ending June 30, the adjusted declared value in the case of a foreign corporation shall be the original declared value adjusted, in accordance with regulations prescribed by the Commissioner with the approval of the Secretary, to reflect increases or decreases (for the period specified in the preceding sentence) in the capital employed in the transaction of its business in the United States.

(*g*) The terms used in this section shall have the same meaning as when used in the Revenue Act of 1932.

SEC. 216. (*a*) There is hereby imposed upon the net income of every corporation, for each income-tax taxable year ending after the close of the first year in respect of which it is taxable under section 215, an excess-profits tax equivalent to 5 per centum of such portion of its net income for such income-tax taxable year as is in excess of 12½ per centum of the adjusted declared value of its capital stock (or in the case of a foreign corporation the adjusted declared value of capital employed in the transaction of its business in the United States) as of the close of the preceding income-tax year (or as of the date of organization if it had no preceding income-tax taxable year) determined as provided in section 215. The terms used in this section shall have the same meaning as when used in the Revenue Act of 1932.

(*b*) The tax imposed by this section shall be assessed, collected, and paid in the same manner, and shall be subject to the same provisions of law (including penalties), as the taxes imposed by Title I of the Revenue Act of 1932.

SEC. 217. (*a*) The President shall proclaim the date of—

(1) the close of the first fiscal year ending June 30 of any year after the year 1933, during which the total receipts

of the United States (excluding public-debt receipts) exceed its total expenditures (excluding public-debt expenditures other than those chargeable against such receipts), or

(2) the repeal of the eighteenth amendment to the Constitution,

whichever is the earlier.

(*b*) Effective as of the 1st day of the calendar year following the date so proclaimed section 617 (a) of the Revenue Act of 1932, as amended, is amended by striking out "1½ cents" and inserting in lieu thereof "1 cent."

(*c*) The tax on dividends imposed by section 213 shall not apply to any dividends declared on or after the 1st day of the calendar year following the date so proclaimed.

(*d*) The capital-stock tax imposed by section 215 shall not apply to any taxpayer in respect of any year beginning on or after the 1st day of July following the date so proclaimed.

(*e*) The excess-profits tax imposed by section 216 shall not apply to any taxpayer in respect of any taxable year after its taxable year during which the date so proclaimed occurs.

SEC. 218. (*a*) Effective as of January 1, 1933, sections 117, 23 (i), 169, 187, and 205 of the Revenue Act of 1932 are repealed.

(*b*) Effective as of January 1, 1933, section 23 (r) (2) of the Revenue Act of 1932 is repealed.

(*c*) Effective as of January 1, 1933, section 23 (r) (3) of the Revenue Act of 1932 is amended by striking out all after the word "Territory" and inserting a period.

(*d*) Effective as of January 1, 1933, section 182 (a) of the Revenue Act of 1932 is amended by inserting at the end thereof a new sentence as follows: "No part of any loss disallowed to a partnership as a deduction by section 23 (r) shall be allowed as a deduction to a member of such partnership in computing net income."

(*e*) Effective as of January 1, 1933, section 141 (c) of the Revenue Act of 1932 is amended by striking out "except that for the taxable years 1932 and 1933 there shall be added to the rate of tax prescribed by sections 13 (a), 201 (b), and 204 (a), a rate of three fourths of 1 per centum" and inserting in lieu thereof the following: "except that for the taxable years 1932 and 1933 there shall be added to the rate of tax prescribed by sections 12 (a), 201 (b), and 204 (a), a rate of three fourths of 1 per centum and except that for the taxable years 1934 and 1935 there shall be added to the rate of tax prescribed by sections 13 (a), 201 (b), and 204 (a), a rate of 1 per centum."

(*f*) No interest shall be assessed or collected for any period prior to September 15, 1933, upon such portion of any amount determined as a deficiency in income taxes as is attributable solely to the amendments made to the Revenue Act of 1932 by this section.

(*g*) In cases where the effect of this section is to require for a taxable year ending prior to June 30, 1933, the making of an income-tax return not otherwise required by law, the time for making the return and paying the tax shall be the same as if the return was for a fiscal year ending June 30, 1933.

(*h*) Section 55 of the Revenue Act of 1932 is amended by inserting before the period at the end thereof a semicolon and the following: "and all returns made under this Act after the date of enactment of the National Industrial Recovery Act shall constitute public records and shall be open to public examination and inspection to such extent as shall be authorized in rules and regulations promulgated by the President."

SEC. 219. Section 500 (*a*) (1) of the Revenue Act of 1926, as amended, is amended by striking out the period at the end of the second sentence thereof and inserting in lieu thereof a comma and the following: "except that no tax shall be imposed in the case of persons admitted free to any spoken play (not a mechanical reproduction), whether or not set to music or with musical parts or accompaniment, which is a consecutive narrative interpreted by a single set of characters, all necessary to the development of the plot, in two or more acts, the performance consuming more than 1 hour and 45 minutes of time."

APPROPRIATION

SEC. 220. For the purposes of this Act, there is hereby authorized to be appropriated, out of any money in the Treasury not otherwise appropriated, the sum of $3,300,000,000. The President is authorized to allocate so much of said sum, not in excess of $100,000,000, as he may determine to be necessary for expenditures in carrying out the Agricultural Adjustment Act and the purposes, powers, and functions heretofore and hereafter conferred upon the Farm Credit Administration.

SEC. 221. Section 7 of the Agricultural Adjustment Act, approved May 12, 1933, is amended by striking out all of its present terms and provisions and substituting therefor the following:

"SEC. 7. The Secretary shall sell the cotton held by him at his discretion, but subject to the foregoing provisions: *Provided,* That he shall dispose of all cotton held by him by March 1, 1936: *Provided further,* That, notwithstanding the provisions of section 6, the Secretary shall have authority to enter into option contracts with producers of cotton to sell to the producers such cotton held by him, in such amounts and at such prices and upon such terms and conditions as the Secretary may deem advisable, in combination with rental or benefit payments provided for in part 2 of this title.

"Notwithstanding any provisions of existing law, the Secretary of Agriculture may in the administration of the Agricultural Adjustment Act make public such information as he deems necessary in order to effectuate the purposes of such Act."

TITLE III—AMENDMENTS TO EMERGENCY RELIEF AND CONSTRUCTION ACT AND MISCELLANEOUS PROVISIONS

SEC. 301. After the expiration of ten days after the date upon which the Administrator has qualified and taken office, (1) no application shall be approved by the Reconstruction Finance Corporation under the provisions of subsection (a) of section 201 of the Emergency Relief and Construction Act of 1932, as amended, and (2) the Administrator shall have access to all applications, files, and records of the

Reconstruction Finance Corporation relating to loans and contracts and the administration of funds under such subsection: *Provided,* that the Reconstruction Finance Corporation may issue funds to a borrower under such subsection (a) prior to January 23, 1939, under the terms of any agreement or any commitment to bid upon or purchase bonds entered into with such borrower pursuant to an application approved prior to the date of termination, under this section, of the power of the Reconstruction Finance Corporation to approve applications.

DECREASE OF BORROWING POWER OF RECONSTRUCTION FINANCE CORPORATION

SEC. 302. The amount of notes, debentures, bonds, or other such obligations which the Reconstruction Finance Corporation is authorized and empowered under section 9 of the Reconstruction Finance Corporation Act, as amended, to have outstanding at any one time is decreased by $400,000,000.

SEPARABILITY CLAUSE

SEC. 303. If any provision of this Act, or the application thereof to any person or circumstances, is held invalid, the remainder of the Act, and the application of such provision to other persons or circumstances, shall not be affected thereby.

SHORT TITLE

SEC. 304. This Act may be cited as the "National Industrial Recovery Act."

Passed the House of Representatives May 26, 1933.
Attest: SOUTH TRIMBLE,
Clerk.

Passed the Senate, with amendments, June 6 (calendar day, June 9), 1933.
Attest: EDWIN A. HALSEY,
Secretary.

Approved, June 16, 1933, 11:55 A.M.

APPENDIX III

STATEMENT BY THE PRESIDENT OUTLINING GENERAL POLICIES OF ADMINISTRATION TO BE PUT INTO EFFECT UNDER THE RECOVERY ACT

JUNE 16, 1933

THE law I have just signed was passed *to put people back to work* — to let them buy more of the products of farms and factories and start our business at a living rate again. This task is in two stages — first, to get many hundreds of thousands of the unemployed back on the payroll by snowfall and second, to plan for a better future for the longer pull. While we shall not neglect the second, the first stage is an emergency job. It has the right of way.

The second part of the act gives employment by a vast program of public works. Our studies show that we should be able to hire many men at once and to step up to about a million new jobs by October 1st, and a much greater number later. We must put at the head of our list those works which are fully ready to start now. Our first purpose is to create employment as fast as we can but we should not pour money into unproved projects.

We have worked out our plans for action. Some of it will start tomorrow. I am making available four hundred million dollars for State roads under regulations which I have just signed and I am told that the States will get this work under way at once. I have also just over $200,000,000 for the Navy to start building ships under the London Treaty.

In my inaugural I laid down the simple proposition that nobody is going to starve in this country. It seems to me to be equally plain that no business which depends for existence on paying less than living wages to its workers has any right to continue in this country. By "business" I mean the whole of commerce as well as the whole of industry; by workers I mean all workers — the white collar class as well as the men in overalls; and by *living* wages I mean more than a bare subsistence level—I mean the wages of *decent* living.

Throughout industry, the change from starvation wages and starvation employment to living wages and sustained employment can, in large part, be made by an industrial covenant to which all employers shall subscribe. It is greatly to their interest to do this because decent living, widely spread among our 125,000,000 people eventually means the opening up to industry of the richest market which the world has known. It is the only way to utilize the so-called excess capacity of our industrial plants. This is the principle that makes this one of the most important laws that ever came from Congress because, before the passage of this Act, no such industrial covenant was possible.

On this idea, the first part of the Act proposes to our industry a great spontaneous cooperation to put millions of men back in their regular jobs this summer. The idea is simply for employers to hire more men to do the existing work by reducing the work-hours of each man's week and at the same time paying a living wage for the shorter week.

No employer and no group of less than all employers in a single trade could do this alone and continue to live in business competition. But if *all* employers in each trade now band themselves faithfully in these modern guilds—without exception—and agree to act together and at once, none will be hurt and millions of workers, so long deprived of the right to earn their bread in the sweat of their labor, can raise their heads again. The challenge of this law is whether we can sink selfish interest and present a solid front against a common peril.

It is a challenge to industry which has long insisted that, given the right to act in unison, it could do much for the general good which has hitherto been unlawful. From today it has that right.

Many good men voted this new charter with misgivings. I do not share these doubts. I had part in the great co-operation of 1917 and 1918 and it is my faith that we can count on our industry once more to join in our general purpose to lift this new threat and to do it without taking any advantage of the public trust which has this day been reposed without stint in the good faith and high purpose of American business.

But industry is challenged in another way. It is not only the slackers within trade groups who may stand in the path of our common purpose. In a sense these groups compete with each other, and no single industry, and no separate cluster of industries, can do this job alone for exactly the same reason that no single employer can do it alone. In other words, we can imagine such a thing as a *slacker industry*.

This law is also a challenge to labor. Workers, too, are here given a new charter of rights long sought and hitherto denied. But they know that the first move expected by the nation is a great cooperation of all employers, by one single mass-action, to improve the case of workers on a scale never attempted in any nation. Industries can do this only if they have the support of the whole public and especially of their own workers. This is not a law to foment discord and it will not be executed as such. This is a time for mutual confidence and help and we can safely rely on the sense of fair play among all Americans to assure every industry which now moves forward promptly in this united drive against depression that its workers will be with it to a man.

It is, further, a challenge to administration. We are relaxing some of the safeguards of the anti-trust laws. The public must be protected against the abuses that led to their enactment, and to this end, we are putting in place of old principles of unchecked competition some new government controls. They must above all be impartial and just. Their purpose is to free business—not to shackle it—and no man who stands on the constructive forward-looking side of his industry has anything to fear from them. To such men the opportunities for individual initiative will open more amply than ever. Let me make it clear, however, that the anti-trust laws still stand firmly against monopolies that restrain trade and price fixing which allows inordinate profits or unfairly high prices.

If we ask our trade groups to do that which exposes their business, as never before, to undermining by members who are unwilling to do their parts, we must guard those who play the game for the general good against those who may seek selfish gains from the unselfishness of others. We must protect them from the racketeers who invade organizations of both employers and workers. We are spending billions of dollars and if that spending is really to serve our ends it must be done quickly. We must see that our haste does not permit favoritism and graft. All this is a heavy load for any Government and one that can be borne only if we have the patience, cooperation, and support of people everywhere.

Finally, this law is a challenge to our whole people. There is no power in America that can force against the public will such action as we require. But there is no group in America that can withstand the force of an aroused public opinion. This great cooperation can succeed only if those who bravely go forward to restore jobs have aggressive public support and those who lag are made to feel the full weight of public disapproval.

As to the machinery—the practical way of accomplishing what we are setting out to do, when a trade association has a code ready to submit and the association has qualified as truly representative, and after reasonable notice has been issued to all concerned, a public hearing will be held by the Administrator or a deputy. A Labor Advisory Board appointed by the Secretary of Labor will be responsible that every affected labor group, whether organized or unorganized, is fully and adequately represented in an advisory capacity and any interested labor group will be entitled to be heard through representatives of its own choosing. An Industrial Advisory Board appointed by the Secretary of Commerce will be responsible that every affected industrial group is fully and adequately represented in an advisory capacity and any interested industrial group will be entitled to be heard through representatives of its own choosing. A Consumers Advisory Board will be responsible that the interests of the consuming public will be represented and every reasonable opportunity will be given to any group or class who may be affected directly or indirectly to present their views.

At the conclusion of these hearings and after the most

careful scrutiny by a competent economic staff the Administrator will present the subject to me for my action under the law.

I am fully aware that wage increases will eventually raise costs, but I ask that managements give first consideration to the improvement of operating figures by greatly increased sales to be expected from the rising purchasing power of the public. That is good economics and good business. The aim of this whole effort is to restore our rich domestic market by raising its vast consuming capacity. If we now inflate prices as fast and as far as we increase wages, the whole project will be set at naught. We cannot hope for the full effect of this plan unless, in these first critical months, and, even at the expense of full initial profits, we defer price increases as long as possible. If we can thus start a strong sound upward spiral of business activity our industries will have little doubt of black-ink operations in the last quarter of this year. The pent-up demand of this people is very great and if we can release it on so broad a front, we need not fear a lagging recovery. There is greater danger of too much feverish speed.

In a few industries, there has been some forward buying at unduly depressed prices in recent weeks. Increased costs resulting from this Government-inspired movement may make it very hard for some manufacturers and jobbers to fulfill some of their present contracts without loss. It will be a part of this wide industrial cooperation for those having the benefit of these forward bargains (contracted before the law was passed) to take the initiative in revising them to absorb some share of the increase in their suppliers' costs, thus raised in the public interest. It is only in such a willing and considerate spirit, throughout the whole of industry, that we can hope to succeed.

Under Title I of this Act, I have appointed Hugh Johnson as Administrator and a special Industrial Recovery Board under the Chairmanship of the Secretary of Commerce. This organization is now prepared to receive proposed Codes and to conduct prompt hearings looking toward their submission to me for approval. While acceptable proposals of no trade group will be delayed, it is my hope that the ten major industries which control the bulk of industrial employment can submit their simple basic Codes at once and that the country can look forward to the month of July as the beginning of our great national movement back to work.

During the coming three weeks Title II relating to public works and construction projects will be temporarily conducted by Colonel Donald H. Sawyer as Administrator and a special temporary board consisting of the Secretary of the Interior as Chairman, the Secretary of Commerce, the Secretary of Agriculture, the Secretary of War, the Attorney General, the Secretary of Labor and the Director of the Budget.

During the next two weeks the Administrator and this board will make a study of all projects already submitted or to be submitted and, as previously stated, certain allotments under the new law will be made immediately.

Between these twin efforts—public works and industrial re-employment—it is not too much to expect that a great many men and women can be taken from the ranks of the unemployed before winter comes. It is the most important attempt of this kind in history. As in the great crisis of the World War, it puts a whole people to the simple but vital test:—*"Must we go on in many groping, disorganized, separate units to defeat or shall we move as one great team to victory?"*

APPENDIX IV

NATIONAL RECOVERY ADMINISTRATION

(Bulletin 2, June 19, 1933)

BASIC CODES OF FAIR COMPETITION

(1) This bulletin is intended to inform all trade association, industrial, and labor groups how to proceed to secure the benefits of the National Industrial Recovery Act. In his statement upon the signing of the act, the President said with reference to prompt submission of codes of fair competition:

"This organization is now prepared to receive proposed codes and to conduct prompt hearings looking toward their submission to me for approval. While acceptable proposals of no trade group will be delayed it is my hope that the 10 major industries which control the bulk of industrial employment can submit their simple basic codes at once and that the country can look forward to the month of July as the beginning of our great national movement back to work."

This bulletin covers the procedure necessary to comply with the President's suggestion.

(2) The National Recovery Administration will receive proposed codes at any time after this date at its office in the Department of Commerce Building, Washington, D. C. Codes may be submitted by mail and will be promptly examined and associations or groups submitting them will be given such suggestions as are appropriate for further action. Consistent with the President's statement, the major industries will so far as practical have the first attention of the Administrator.

As soon as the proposed code is put in proper form, after consultation with those submitting it, due public notice will be given of a date for a hearing on the code, and at such hearing a reasonable opportunity to be heard will be given to all interested parties, including all affected labor groups, and representatives of consumer organizations, the trade associations or groups submitting codes and any essen-

safeguards for the health and safety of the workers and for stabilization of their employment.

(*d*) The following principle emphasized in the President's statement should be recognized and adhered to:

"I am fully aware that wage increases will eventually raise costs, but I ask that managements give first consideration to the improvement of operating figures by greatly increased sales to be expected from the rising purchasing power of the public. That is good economics and good business. The aim of this whole effort is to restore our rich domestic market by raising its vast consuming capacity. If we now inflate prices as fast and as far as we increase wages, the whole project will be set at naught. We cannot hope for the full effect of this plan unless, in these first critical months, and, even at the expense of full initial profits, we defer price increases as long as possible."

In the drafting of codes, attention is especially directed to this suggestion by the President that the recovery administration cannot be effective unless the consumer's buying power is protected. There will be full protection for the consumer. The codes should recognize the interest of the public in the matter of prices.

(8) At the hearing described in paragraph 2 every trade association or group proposing a code should be prepared to establish by evidence the requirements of section 3 (a), clause 1, of the act which provides: That such associations or groups impose no inequitable restrictions on admission to membership therein and are truly representative to such trades or industries or subdivisions thereof, and of section 3 (a), clause 2, of the act which provides: That such code or codes are not designed to promote monopolies or to eliminate or oppress small enterprises and will not operate to discriminate against them, and will tend to effectuate the policy of this title.

(9) It is the purpose of the act to encourage a voluntary submission of codes of fair competition and the procedure offered by these provisions for basic codes is intended to simplify and expedite this process. But in the event that codes of fair competition are not voluntarily submitted, attention is invited to other pertinent provisions of the act.

It is provided in section 3 (d) of the act that the President upon his own motion or if complaint is made, may after public notice and hearing prescribe a code of fair competition for a trade or industry or subdivision thereof. Section 3 (d) reads as follows:

Upon his own motion, or if complaint is made to the President that abuses inimical to the public interest and contrary to the policy herein declared are prevalent in any trade or industry or subdivision thereof, and if no code of fair competition thereof has theretofore been approved by the President, the President, after such public notice and hearing as he shall specify, may prescribe and approve a code of fair competition for such trade or industry or subdivision thereof, which shall have the same effect as a code of fair competition approved by the President under subsection (a) of this section.

In this same connection, attention should be directed to the requirements of sections 7 (b) and (c), which read as follows:

The President shall, so far as practicable, afford every opportunity to employers and employees in any trade or industry or subdivision thereof with respect to which the conditions referred to in clauses (1) and (2) of subsection (a) prevail to establish by mutual agreement, the standards as to the maximum hours of labor, minimum rates of pay, and such other conditions of employment as may be necessary in such trade or industry or subdivision thereof to effectuate the policy of this title; and the standards established in such agreements, when approved by the President, shall have the same effect as a code of fair competition, approved by the President under subsection (a) of section 3.

(*c*) Where no such mutual agreement has been approved by the President he may investigate the labor practices, policies, wages, hours of labor, and conditions of employment in such trade or industry or subdivision thereof; and upon the basis of such investigations, and after such hearings as the President finds advisable, he is authorized to prescribe a limited code of fair competition fixing such maximum hours of labor, minimum rates of pay, and other conditions of employment in the trade or industry or subdivision thereof investigated as he finds to be necessary to effectuate the policy of this title, which shall have the same effect as a code of fair competition approved by the President under subsection (a) of section 3. The President may differentiate according to experience and skill of the employees affected and according to the locality of employment; but no attempt shall be made to introduce any classification according to the nature of the work involved which might tend to set a maximum as well as a minimum wage.

Under the foregoing provision of the act if no code or agreement establishing standards as to maximum hours of labor, minimum rates of pay, and conditions of employment has been approved by the President, the President is authorized under the foregoing section (7) (c) to prescribe a limited code upon the basis of such investigations and after such hearings as he finds advisable.

HUGH S. JOHNSON,
Administrator.

Approved by:

National Industrial Recovery Board.

Hon. Daniel C. Roper, Chairman.
Hon. Homer S. Cummings.
Hon. Harold L. Ickes.
Hon. Henry A. Wallace.
Hon. Frances Perkins.
Hon. Charles H. March.
Hon. Lewis W. Douglas.
Hon. John Dickinson, Executive Secretary.

TABLE OF JUDICIAL DECISIONS

CITED IN TEXT

INDEX

O

P

Barnes & Noble
12-6-34